Practical Magic

Practical Magic

A book of transformations, spells & mind magic

Marian Green

LORENZ BOOKS

First published in 2001 by Lorenz Books

Lorenz Books is an imprint of
Anness Publishing Limited
Hermes House
88–89 Blackfriars Road
London SE1 8HA

Published in the USA by Lorenz Books,
Anness Publishing Inc., 27 West 20th Street,
New York, NY 10011

www.lorenzbooks.com

This edition distributed in Canada by
Raincoast Books, 9050 Shaughnessy Street
Vancouver, British Columbia V6P 6E5

A CIP catalogue record for this book is available
from the British Library

Publisher: Joanna Lorenz
Senior Editor: Joanne Rippin
Design: SteersMcGillan Limited
Special Photography: Don Last and
    Michelle Garrett

Production Controller: Don Campaniello
Editorial reader: Richard McGinlay
Typesetter: Diane Pullen

10 9 8 7 6 5 4 3

PICTURE ACKNOWLEDGEMENTS

AKG, London: p6BL *Astronomie: Geschichte*. p24L *Preparations for the Wedding of the Sultans Daughter* by Jose Tapiro y Baro, p26TR *The Cemetery* by Caspar David Friedrich. p27BR *Island of the Dead*. p28TR *Investiture of the First Grand Master of the Order of St George*, Erich Lessing. p29B *Templar Trials 1305-1313 from Chroniques de France*. p35BR *Hecate* by William Blake. p36TR *Apollo with the Hours* by Georg Friedrich Kersting. p36B *Sun Deities*, wallpainting from a tomb, Egypt. p40BR *Palais du Tau, Reims*. p55BL Hexenritt. p46TR *Journey of Sun God*. p53BR *Junotempel in Agrigent* by Caspar David Friedrich. p60T *L'atmosphere meteorologie populaire* from Camille Flammarion. p62B *Rebecca and Elijah at the Well*. p74BL Erich Lessing. p88MR *Appolontempel, John Hios*. p89M *Delphic Oracle*. p89TR *Apparition in the Woods* by Moritz von Schwind. **Bridgeman Art Library, London**: p6TR *The Sorceress* by Henry Meynell Rheam. p7R *The Alchemist* . p12L *Pan and Psyche* by Sir Edward Burne-Jones. p12R *Diana the Huntress* by Gaston Casimir Saintpierre. p22BL *Archangel Gabriel* by Sandro Botticelli. p28B *Grand Conventional Festival of the Britons* after Charles Hamilton Smith. p30T *Assembly of Freemasons to Initiate an Apprentice*, French School. p30B *Chapter of the Order of the Templars, Paris, 22nd April 1147* by Marius Granet. p31B *Dionyiac Mystery Cult*, Villa dei Misteri, Italy. p34T *Luna* by Evelyn de Morgan. p38 Astrological calendar. p39TR Eastern Zodiac Chart. p50/51 *The Spell* by William Fettes Douglas. p55T *Visit to the Witch* by Edward Frederick Brewtnall. p58T *Circe Offering the Cup to Ulysses* by John William Waterhouse. p62TR *St Guthlac Ordained Priest* by Bishop Hedda.

p68BM *May Day Garlands* by Thomas Falcon Marshall. p70BR *Cottage Industry* by William Hincks (after). p71BM *St Michael weighing souls at the Last Judgement* by Rogier van der Weyden. p76T *The Weighing of the Heart against the Feather of Truth* from The Book of the Dead of the Scribe Ani. p77BL *The Garden at Vetheuil* by Monet. p89BR *Angel* by Sir Edward Burne-Jones. **Collections**: p68MR G. Burns. P69BR Glyn Davies. **David Noble**, Kent: p34B. p52BL. p67TR. p72B **E.T. Archive, London**: p31TR *Mystic rites* from The Astrologer (1825). p39TL *Love under influence of Venus-Taurus* De Sphaera manuscript. P39B Scholium de Duodecim Zodiac. p77T Historia Naturalis by Pliny the Elder. p88M. Edmund Nägele **FRPS**: p10T. **Fortean Picture Library**: p32, 43BL, 48B Andrew Stewart. p87TL, 87BL Peter Mandel/Dr Elmar R. Gruber. p88BR Derek Stafford. **Galaxy Picture Library**: p69M Robin Scagell. **Genesis Space Photo Library**: p40T. p41B. **The Hutchison Library**: p74BR Liba Taylor. **Images Colour Library**: p69T David Brown. **Mary Evans Picture Library, London**: p22TR *King Arthur asks the Lady of the Lake for Excalibur* by Walter Crane. **Mick Sharp Photography**: p71MR, p73MR Jean Williamson.. **Robert Harding Picture Library**: p8. p13BR Frans Lanting. p23MR Douglas Peebles. p23BR Adam Woolfitt. p27BL Tony Waltham. p52T. **Sylvia Cordaiy Photo Library Ltd**: p13BL **Nick Rains Photography**. p23BL Guy Marks. p49BL Chris Taylor. p49BR John Parker. **Skyscan Photo library**: p13T. p36TL. **Tony Stone Images**: p64/65 David Loftus. p71M Hans Strand. Travel Ink: p11TL Leslie Garland. p29T Nick Battersby. p23ML David Martyn Hughes. p47T Charcrit Boonsom.

Contents

Introduction

The words "magic" and "witchcraft" have a wonderful ring to them, yet it is possible to think that they are subjects which have no part in modern life. The truth is that there are as many practising witches and magicians now as there have ever been. It may seem that their knowledge is strange and mysterious, yet they are using natural powers anyone can develop. It has long been known that the gravity of the Moon and Sun affects life on Earth, and the old witches and magicians tried to work with these changing forces, to see into the future, to bring about change for good, and to heal. Using plants, candles and ribbons, the old ways can be adapted for today's needs, and the same forces which bring the cycle of passing seasons, the growth and repose of Nature, can be used in our lives too.

The aim of this book

This is to show readers that the arts and crafts of the wise people of old are still valid, even though we have just entered a new era, the Age of Aquarius, and left behind the Age of Pisces (see below). While methods of communication have advanced greatly with time, what it is we communicate about has not changed as much – we still have to find ways of talking to the Gods, Goddesses, Angels and powers who lie behind the success of magic, be it ancient or modern. No matter how advanced some of our discoveries may

be, archaeologists, historians and seekers are still trying to unravel the mysteries left to us by the wise ones of Ancient Egypt, South America, the Far East and Europe. They may sift the soil from ancient graves, decipher hieroglyphs, and reconstruct buildings, but they cannot enter the minds of those who lie in the graves, who wrote the hieroglyphs, who laid out and constructed the pyramids or the vast stone temples all over the world. These tasks may well be best left to the magician, working on the verge of the Age of Aquarius, when the same stars that shone on the birth of humanity now align to a new configuration. We have now left the Age of Pisces, when people acted together like schools of fish; the symbol of Aquarius is the lone Water Bearer, bringing life-giving water to all who need it. Like the Holy Grail, which is still a Mystery, this water container may hold the wine of ancient wisdom, poured out from the eternal yet restless stars. Anyone can drink, if they can reach up and out to touch the flow of eternal water, using the skills, arts and crafts of magic, which are as old as the hills themselves.

This book consists of beautiful and evocative images which will awaken insights through meditation, as well as mental, magical and practical exercises, and what might be called "spiritual" or "psychic" techniques. These are designed to awaken perceptions and senses that have been blunted by living in a modern, stressful world. Many of them may seem rather

△ **A magician calls the forces of Nature into a healing potion.**

△ **A witch uses her wand to summon the power of the Elements.**

WITCHES

Following the ancient arts of Natural magic, witches use the seasons and tides of the Earth, Moon and Sun to strengthen their spells. They are pagans, worshipping a Great Mother Goddess and a horned or solar God, although there are many pagan deities honoured by modern pagans. They have a cycle of sacred celebrations throughout the year, and they also work with the energy of the full Moon. Some witches work as individuals, performing their rituals alone. Others are members of a family or tradition. Some witches celebrate the seasons or make magic alone while others are initiated into covens, and share meetings and festivals with a group throughout the sacred year.

MAGICIANS

Ceremonial or ritual magicians, which include both men and women, usually follow one of the aspects of the Western Mystery Tradition which goes back to the time of Hermes Trismegistus in Ancient Egypt.

There are several basic schools of magicians. Many follow the Qabalah, an ancient Hebrew mystical tradition of which there are at least three branches: the Jewish; the Christian, and the mystical or magical Qabalah. Others work with the Arthurian legends and the Holy Grail, or the Celtic, Greek, Roman or Egyptian traditions. Each of these provides a framework of symbols, mythological stories of the Gods and Goddesses, magical practices and a great body of inherited wisdom.

There are training schools and lodges of magicians, who are far fewer than the witches and wiccans. Many magicians are involved with research, developing new magical techniques as we leave the Age of Pisces and enter the Age of Aquarius.

△ The tools of the magician, including Tarot cards and symbols of the Elements.

△ **The powers of the stars and planets have always been called upon in magic.**

WICCANS

Wicca is a modern form of witchcraft that was developed in the 19th century. Wiccans are usually members of a coven, or group, that is led by a High Priestess and High Priest. There will have been some kind of initiation into this form of witchcraft. They have a series of rituals and prayers which are written down in what is sometimes called a Book of Shadows.

Many of their ceremonies were reconstructed and published in the 1950s by Gerald Gardner and Doreen Valiente. All covens are independent and follow their own paths.

strange at first, if you have never consciously tried to alter your state of awareness, but all are quite safe. You may think it odd that you are advised to break old habits, but the objective of all these practices is to be in total control of your own being. It is often easier to go along, scarcely aware of what is going on around you, acting out of habit with willpower completely asleep.

If you wish to improve your world, you need to strengthen your willpower – the comfort of following others or acting automatically, will have to go. Take a grip of all your activities – physical, mental and spiritual – and you will soon discover what you have been missing all these years.

One has to learn to develop the necessary magical powers – and they can be improved with practice. Using a few simple objects, which reflect a long tradition of occult symbolism, you can make a sacred place, set out an altar and awaken those sleeping powers of creativity from within. Everyone has many talents that they never exploit. Anyone can learn to play a musical instrument if they choose, but they need to practise and master the skills by continued work. Magic is the same.

Magic, Witchcraft and Sorcery

The paths of magic are
available for anyone to follow,
be they the winding road of
the country witch, the hard
road of ceremonial magic,
or the inner way of the
sorcerer or shaman.
All use symbols, ritual acts
and the development of
inner power.

Rediscovery of the
Old Skills

Although the arts of magic are very old, they are quite simple, and can be mastered by people who have a little patience and application. Two basic skills which need to be understood are Meditation and Creative Visualisation, both of which increase Concentration. Concentration helps you to focus on the desire of the spell or ritual, and it is this that makes it happen.

Then the arts of Ritual need to be understood for these provide the impetus to make the magic work, and there needs to be some kind of Spiritual or Religious belief to call on for help with our requests and invocations. Ritual uses the practical skills of making items, setting out altars and gathering seasonal symbols, while a spiritual belief has to be sought from within, and made real through communication with your chosen pantheon of deities.

MEDITATING ON THE SEASONS

△ **Spring brings awakening.**

△ **Autumn grants an inner harvest.**

△ **Summer offers fulfilment.**

△ **Winter bestows repose.**

The arts of magic can be briefly defined as methods of causing coincidences to happen. By defining a need, focusing on it, using ancient symbols, from Nature in witchcraft, or from more intellectual sources in ceremonial magic, a pattern is created. That pattern is first made in the world of imagination and creativity, but by speaking a spell or working a ritual, it is brought into our own world reality. Some arts are complicated, others are just ways of mentally focusing on what needs to be achieved.

Meditation

The first art to look at is Meditation. Meditation is a way of stilling the conscious mind, dismissing everyday concerns from your awareness, and allowing the deeper, more subtle senses to awake and inform your conscious mind. Arts of meditation are part of many ancient religions and many cultures in both the East and the West. It is best to follow a single path within either the Eastern or the Western practice, and not mix them.

Meditation early in the morning is generally better than sessions late at night, but if you have time during the day a quarter of an hour of relaxation and study can be

△ **Meditation is the best gateway to inner wisdom, find time every day to increase your ability.**

△ The quiet of dawn is always the best time for meditation on memories or inspiring images, such as this.

extremely beneficial. Whatever you do, don't merely slump into bed and expect to receive revelations as you nod off. Your results will only become reliable if you persist with regular experiments, so try to have a session, not exceeding 15 minutes, for six out of seven days a week for a couple of months. Meditations will become more and more rewarding, and form a part of all true modern witches' and magicians' daily lives.

Meditation is used to put you in touch first with your inner sense of power and creativity, and later with the Gods and Goddesses, angels and elemental beings which are the partners of witches and magicians in their rituals. Unless you can withdraw from the everyday world for a few minutes each day there is no way that these inner forces can get in touch with you. It is really controlled, conscious dreaming, yet it is also real.

THE THREE "Ss" OF MEDITATION
There are three things that make meditation easier.

1 The first is Stillness. If you sit relaxed and completely still, this helps you to drift into the poised state of awareness where inner material can begin to flow. As soon as you start to wriggle about, or become aware that you are not comfortable you will break the stream of concentration.

2 Silence is also really important. Many people try to use a personal stereo, playing music to blot out any sounds in the environment which they consider will disturb their meditations, but it is far better to find a quiet time of day and learn to create inner silence. This does matter because as well as seeing images many people also hear sounds, and any music will make this much harder. The more you focus on the theme and allow images or feelings to surface, the less you will be distracted. A teacher once said that when you can meditate on a railway platform in the rush hour without being distracted, then you can meditate.

3 Sensitivity is the third skill that you will need to employ. When you begin any new technique it may be difficult to get it to work, and sensitivity may not be obvious. You need to listen, watch and perceive whatever images, sounds, symbols or other sensations start to occur in your mind. These will be vague and fleeting to begin with, but the more still you become, and the quieter the background noises, the sharper your own awareness will become. It does take practice.

SPHERE OF PROTECTION
You may find it helps your concentration if you create a sphere of protection.

The simplest way is to see yourself within a bubble of light, like a large soap bubble, large enough to contain you and some space all round you.

It may take a few sessions of practice to get the clear feeling of a sphere being formed to enclose you safely. If you do this at least once each day, gradually it will strengthen your own aura.

1 Sit on your chair and imagine or mentally create a ball of white fire about a metre (1 yard) in front of you. See it spinning and glowing strongly.

2 See it begin to expand. You will find that it surrounds you, below your feet and above your head, enclosing you in a sphere of brilliant, rainbow light like a transparent bubble.

3 Imagine it strongly, so that you can feel it, almost smell a favourite perfume, or really see the transparent, rainbow-hued globe gently enclosing you.

The aim is to purify the area around you when you are meditating, or later performing magical work. Stray thoughts, worries or left-over problems will be kept at bay by this technique, so that what you perceive will be a clear vision.

Gods, Goddesses and
Sacred Places

One of the things that attracts many people to the old arts is a new approach to spirituality of a very personal sort. Many have become disillusioned by organized religions, their dogma and rules, and have sought a more individual and less regulated direction. Some have discovered the new forms of paganism that are springing up all over the world. These new impulses do not try to negate established faiths, but rather discover an older current of belief and practice that runs below them.

△ **The goddess Diana is called on as the protector of wild, natural places.**

Gods and Goddesses

Belief in Gods and Goddesses often originates from the pagan religions of ancient times which acknowledged a male and a female aspect of deity, often seen as the Sky Father and the Earth Mother. In classical paganism these two energies were further divided into whole pantheons of Goddesses and Gods, each with their own powers and specialities.

In many traditions the Sun is a male god of light, and the Moon a goddess with either three faces or three phases with different names. These deities are encountered in many ancient religions, and those who are drawn to modern paganism are finding a wealth of images and ideas to contemplate. No one is forced to become a pagan; it has to be a path found by each seeker, and each one has to understand it for themselves. All witches and wiccans are pagans; but not all pagans are witches or wiccans. It is possible to be a pagan druid, a pagan follower of the Norse gods and goddesses, or a pagan worshipper of the gods of Ancient Egypt, Greece or Rome, or of many of the ancient deities of the lands around the globe.

△ **The old Gods can give blessings to those who rediscover and honour them.**

FOLLOWING YOUR OWN PATH

You must discover for yourself a close and living connection to the Creative Spirit, the Goddess, or the Gods of your chosen tradition. It is for this reason that there can't be any pagan or magical religious missionaries.

There is no one book, no set of rules, no gospel truth, no "thou shalt not" type of commandments, except what common sense and common decency suggest. Each individual on the path has to find their own Gods, discover their symbols, and invite them into their life.

△ Constructing sacred circles in the landscape linked Earth and Heaven in ancient times.

Sacred Places

One factor which is important to all workers of magic is the reality of a female force of equal power and worth to a male force. Most modern major religions, apart from Hinduism, pay little heed to female deities and goddesses, yet modern people who are seeking a new spiritual direction have become aware of this lack, and are looking to the ancient world to fill the gap.

In mythology, goddesses do not go away, and unlike their male counterparts they do not die. The goddess lives on, with many names and faces, and it is her companion or lover or son who may die and be reborn. The god is symbolized by the green of Nature, being born in the spring, growing to fullness at midsummer, waning in the autumn and dying, being reborn in winter. It seems that from the very earliest moments of human history people have had a very special relationship with certain places on Earth and with the Sun, Moon and stars. In many lands, the most ancient monuments are not castles or palaces, but temples and sacred groves, caves, and places of burial.

Although it is easier to visit an outdoor site, with all its associations of ancient magic, the neglected hearts of cities and towns are just as important, and can offer healing and a new current of life-giving energy if they are located, cleared out, honoured and

△ Visions of places untouched by humanity offer deep balm for the soul.

acknowledged. Each magician or witch has their own personal awareness of the land and therefore of the places in harmony with it, consequently, there is no formula for finding sacred places. There has to be complete freedom so that everyone can come to terms with their own concepts of higher beings. Much magical practice relies on the powers of the gods, Angels, spirit guides, Elemental beings and other kinds of spirits, who you will come to meet as you go

△ Where river and forest meet, so do the Goddess and the God, giving life to the land.

along. It will be necessary for you to meditate, consider and perhaps walk a path of imagination that will lead you to have some religious experiences of your own. There can be no rights and wrongs in religious belief just as there aren't in the life that you choose to lead or the career that you follow. You must seriously consider the question in the light of your current knowledge, then read and meditate, and later experience things for yourself.

The gift of Nature and

Herbs and their Uses

Herbal medicine has become popular again after many years of neglect. There are plenty of simple herb teas that can be drunk purely for pleasure and relaxation, or to relieve tension, sleeplessness, menstrual problems or fever. You will probably find new uses for the parsley, sage and mint in the garden, for these can help a wide variety of minor ills. New herbs can easily be grown, even in sunny window boxes, or on roofs or patios.

△ Herbs may be used fresh or dried, but should be carefully prepared.

SOME USEFUL HERBS

Feverfew leaves eaten in honey sandwiches can ease migraines, and this daisy-flowered herb with its peppery scent is common, growing wild in some places.

Some teas are mainly refreshing, like lemon balm (Melissa), while others can have medicinal actions, like peppermint (Mentha viridens). Comfrey, dandelions, thyme and camomile are useful, and any good book on herbs will have clear pictures or photographs of these plants so that you can learn to recognize them in the countryside.

Using Herbs

In every land there has been a tradition of plant medicine, sometimes widely known and sometimes kept as secret wisdom by certain members of society. To understand this vast subject fully and use plant material safely will require study and commitment, but some simple teas may be made, or herbal infusions which may be poured into water to bathe in or to rinse your hair.

Any herb which is commonly used either fresh or dried in cooking will be safe to use in small amounts, although you need to learn the special properties of each before attempting to treat any illness. Be very careful that you know exactly which plant you are dealing with if you are going to drink the infusion, or eat it dried in cookery.

Learning About Herbs

Ideally you should find a teacher who can show you how to recognize each plant, where to grow it and how to prepare the various parts of it in the most effective way. Many places now have herb societies which run training courses if you don't have any friends or family members with sufficient knowledge to share with you. There are also some very good correspondence courses available. Once you have established the identity of a plant and what it may be used for, you will need to learn how to prepare it properly for using in your work.

△ **A pestle and mortar are the best utensils to crush seeds and dried herbs.**

USING PLANTS FOR DYEING

Some plants are used for dyeing, including the outside skins of onion or the plant golden rod, which both give yellowish dyes.

The woad plant was famous in ancient times when Celtic tribespeople were painted with blue patterns and it was used more permanently in tattoos. Dyer's Madder (Rubia tinctoria) gives a pinkish red, and many trees, including the twigs of Alder, and Oak galls (Oak apples) have been used to give colour or make ink. Even today there are artists who work by crushing different coloured flower petals to make their pigments.

The skill in dyeing is knowing which plant extract is used with which mordant, a chemical that fixes the colour, so that the results are acceptable.

Making Herbal Teas

Herbal teas are simple to make and need only a pot to brew them in, and possibly a strainer to remove the herb fragments from the drink. Some special teapots have filters inside them so that the fresh or dried herb may be put inside to infuse for a few minutes before use.

Plant material can also be used for:

Tinctures, made in alcohol, producing a stronger dose.

Embrocations, where the liquid is added to some form of grease to be rubbed in, for example, to swollen joints.

Scented or medicinal baths.

Decorating seasonal cakes – the petals of many flowers can be dipped in raw, beaten egg white and then fine sugar to crystallize them.

1 Take a small handful of leaves, recently picked – for most fresh herbs this will make a strong enough infusion. If you have dried herbs, use half the quantity.

2 Rinse the leaves to ensure they are clean. Either tear into small pieces or chop roughly before putting them into the pot.

3 Add boiling water almost to fill the pot. This should be allowed to stand for up to five minutes so that all the goodness, or what the ancients used to call the "virtue", seeps into the water.

4 This may be drunk hot, or warm, or cooled and chilled and used next day. If you are experimenting with this method you will soon learn how much is enough. A lot of traditional wisdom is not measured in grammes or ounces, but in taste and through intuition.

5 Some herbs are quite strange or "medicinal" to the palate. Add honey for sweetness or lemon juice for sharpness to make them more acceptable. Anyone used only to commercially sold teas or herbal tisanes may find those made with fresh herbs are rather stronger and more interesting.

6 Fruit juice may be added to improve the flavour if you like it.

As taste is so personal and each individual's needs different, it is best to experiment for yourself to see what is pleasing, what is effective against minor illnesses, and what can be shared with others to help them.

Herbal Medicine

If you want to use herbal medicine, it is worth getting some proper instruction from one of the herbal societies which exist all over the world. Some offer training by post or at evening classes or weekends.

△ **It is essential to correctly identify any plant you may use.**

You will need some good books, one of which should have clear photographs of the medicinal plants you intend to use so that you can identify what you are dealing with. Another should be an up-to-date herbal which explains the actions of the leaves, fruits, roots or seeds, how they should be prepared and what dosage is used to treat which illness.

A WORD OF WARNING

Never try to use herbs or any other healing method unless you are sure you know what you are doing, and be sure that your plant identification is correct. Parsley, for example, looks very like the poisonous Hemlock (Conium maculatum) so you do need to know which is which. You will also need to learn the Latin names for plants and as many have a wide variety of local names, several different plants are called the same thing in different places. Always use clean equipment, being careful not to mix the mortar in which you grind incenses with one you might use for seeds.

The Arts of Ritual

An important part of most magical ceremonies, rituals are conscious acts that are performed to bring about a specific objective. The tools that are used in ritual, the elements and powers that are invoked, all have particular meaning and significance and must be used with care.

The patterns, power and purpose of

Rituals

Every ritual follows a similar pattern although some systems put more emphasis on one aspect than others. To begin with, it is essential that a clear and precise objective is outlined and that everyone who is involved is fully aware of this purpose, which is often stated at the start of the work. The usual stages rituals need to go through are as follows:

Ritual bathing and robing

If possible, you should always have a bath or shower before a ritual, and if you are able to soak in a warm bath you can add herbs and oils so that you begin to detach yourself from the everyday world. When a group meets this may be difficult, but a ritualized washing of the hands and face will help you to wash away everyday cares and focus on the magic ahead. Ideally you should have a special robe or other magical garment to put on, and as you do so, think about the work you are going to do, calling yourself by your magical name, if you have one, so that it is the initiate or witch who goes into the ritual rather than your everyday self.

Preparing the Place

This may mean clearing space in a room and rearranging the furniture, collecting candles and holders, altar cloths and all the items to go on the altar including bread and wine, flowers, incense, charcoal blocks and any symbols or talisman-making items, for example. If you are able to work out of doors you may still need to set out symbols of the Elements, mark a circle on the ground or define sacred space. You may want to set out altars at the four quarters so that the Elements of Earth, Water, Fire and Air are represented by symbolic objects or candles.

Creating the circle

It is traditional to walk three times clockwise, or sunwise (meaning from East to West via the South), around the sacred space to represent the

ELEMENTAL ALTARS

△ Living fire is usually present during rituals. Fire can also be symbolized by the colour orange, and by yellow or gold flowers.

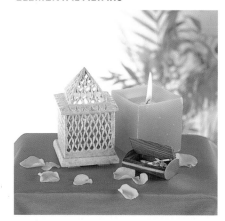

△ Water has many forms, from solid ice to the sacred wine which may be ritually shared. It is also symbolized by the colours blue and green.

△ Air may be symbolized on an altar by incense, scented candles, a fan or feathers and silver-coloured cloth or ornaments.

△ Earth can be symbolized by stone objects and terracotta colours. It is also represented by the bread and salt often used in rituals.

three circles of time and space, or in Qabalistic terms, rings of cosmos, chaos and the ring pass-not. If you are working in a confined space, stand in the centre or near the altar and point with your wand or the first finger of your right hand, and turn round in three circles.

Say aloud the purpose of the ritual, whether it is for divination or a celebration, to consecrate a talisman or work for healing. Everyone should agree to this purpose.

Working the ritual

Calling the Elements: It is usual to call upon the Elements either as guardians, totem animals, archangels or through sacred landscapes. Some people begin with East as sunrise, go on to South as noon, West as sunset and North as midnight, while other people prefer to work through the Elements, starting with Earth in the North, and so on.

Once you have opened the sacred space and stated your purpose, it is necessary to do magically whatever you have decided upon. This could be creating a talisman, or sitting in quiet meditation to receive inner guidance, or enacting a traditional myth, or celebrating a special time of year. This takes as much or as little time as necessary.

△ Bread is broken according to ancient traditions of friendship.

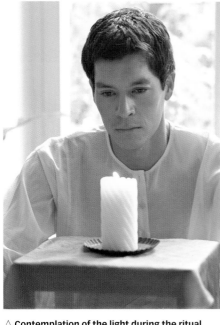

△ Contemplation of the light during the ritual aids its power.

The Communion: It is usual to have a sacred sharing with the physical people in the ritual but also with the Gods or Angels, otherworldly beings or teachers who have been called upon to help with your magic. Something to eat, which may be bread and salt, biscuits, fruit or any other sacred food, placed on a platter, is blessed, often in the name of the Earth Mother who provided it. Then wine, water, milk or any other drink in the chalice is blessed in the name of the Sky God, or by the power of the Sun. The chalice is always taken with both hands to show that everyone is equal and wholly involved.

Closing Meditation: After the communion there is often a pause to meditate on what has been begun by the ritual, or to discuss business or any other matters.

Releasing the Elements: Each quarter is thanked and a reversal of what was said to welcome the powers at the beginning is spoken. Remember you are dealing with beings who are far more powerful than we humans; you cannot command them to come, nor can you demand that they go away. You may only invite them to your circle and give them thanks at the end. Really you may just be awakening to consciousness the inner part of yourself which most closely answers to whoever you are dealing with, and you can't banish part of yourself either.

Unwinding the circles

Walk the three circles anticlockwise (or widdershins, the opposite to sunwise) to bring the place back into harmony with the everyday Earth. You may feel a shift of energy and gentle return to ordinary awareness at this point. When you are clearing up, you might find it useful to discuss the ceremony together. Having a warm drink and something to eat will ensure that everyone is fully grounded and ready to face the world again. Some rituals may only take about half an hour from start to finish, while others can continue for hours, and the sheer effort of concentration during that time can make you extremely hungry.

If you are working for an on-going purpose it is best not to discuss what you have done, so that the magic has time to develop in the silence of secrecy. If it was a festival, then that has been completed and may be shared.

△ Living flames and sweet-scented oils raise the consciousness of the magician.

△ A simple cleansing ritual at the beginning of a gathering purifies those taking part.

The importance and relevance of
Rites, Rituals and Ceremonies

There is possible confusion between three words in this area – rites, rituals and ceremonies. The words "rite" and "ritual" are often interchangeable. Rites tend to have shorter and simpler workings, and are often performed by someone working alone. Much less emphasis is placed on the preparation and the closing of a rite or ritual, with the concentration instead on the central stages. They come in many shapes and forms, and these vary depending on their source or tradition and on their purpose.

A ritual or rite is a conscious act performed to bring about a specific objective – in everyday life these include cleaning your teeth or making a cup of tea. A ceremony, on the other hand, often involves more people, has a more complicated pattern and more elaborate equipment. Ceremonies may be held in public or with an audience.

Individual witches might consider their workings to be rites rather than rituals, as they are far less complicated than those of wiccans or ceremonial magicians. Old-fashioned village witches often celebrated entirely alone or with a close group of family and friends, and as far as possible they would work out of doors. Even today magic workers actually watch the Sun and Moon in the sky, and being out in the open air while performing rites or ceremonies is important to them.

Although wiccan coven members join in esbats at each full moon, these meetings are frequently held indoors, and on a date

△ Witches use the tools of sword, wand, cup and platter during outdoor rites.

PERFORMING A RITE
Each worker of magic will perform rites in their own way, having developed a process that is unique to them. Here is an example of a rite, giving some alternative methods of carrying out the steps.

1 Out of doors, in a secluded place, on your own or in a group, sweep a circle on the ground with a broom, marking a space big enough for the work. You might have a small bonfire at the centre, or candles burning around the edge.

2 Around the circle, which is swept deocil or sunwise, open four gates to the quarters; Earth in the North, Air in the East, Fire in the South and Water in the West. Symbols of the Elements may be placed inside the circle at the East, South and West, but the North is left open so that an open gate remains. Here the broomstick is laid to complete the circle, and to make a way out.

3 At this point you may speak aloud an invocation to call down the power of the Goddess in her relevant phase and the God to enter the circle and be with you during the rite. Power may be raised by chanting, dancing or playing some kind of simple musical instrument. During this part of the rite, which may go on for some time, everyone present focuses on the work in hand, whether it is healing, seeking inspiration, preparing for a divination or acknowledging a greater or lesser festival.

4 Eventually power is collected and sent by a gesture or through a wand to where it is needed. The atmosphere can be felt to change as the energy is sent forth, sometimes seen as a stream of golden sparks.

△ Joss sticks will burn in or out of doors to perfume a working and focus the minds of those sharing it.

5 A communion is shared, which may be bread and wine, then the circle is finally swept again widdershins (in the opposite direction), thanks are spoken and everything cleared away.

A SPELL TO OPEN INNER GATES

Work out why you want to open the gates to inner vision and write the reason down. During a waxing Moon, in the evening, sing this spell.

1 Place a stone, a flower, a small bowl of water and a lighted candle at the four corners of a table. Find a picture of an open door or gate, or draw one.

2 Sit still, relax and focus on your purpose. Stand up and make opening gestures to each of the four quarters. Sing something like the following, picking up each object.

"Open my mind like a growing flower, may my vision now empower.

"Open my mind to the water's flow, that on vision journeys I may go.

"Open my mind to this stone so cold, that visions I shall safely hold."

3 Circle or turn round four times, singing "Open gates that I may roam and bring all my knowledge home."

You will find that your inner visions get clearer each time you do this.

convenient to the members rather than one that is influenced by the moon or stars. Village witches prefer to work on the exact time of the full or new moon, depending on what they are doing. Moon power is very important to witchcraft, for not only is the witch's goddess often seen as a triple-faced moon goddess, but the waxing and waning light of the Moon empowers and has influence over different kinds of magic.

Ceremonies are used by many faiths and movements worldwide to mark special times, to celebrate birth and naming, to join two people formally in marriage, and to lay to rest those who have passed through the gates of death. There are also festivals that tell the stories of the life of the Gods or the Messiah within the tradition.

Some of the ceremonies are led by the priesthood before a congregation while others allow the wider participation of the faithful, in processions, public offerings, hymn singing or ritual dance.

It may take time to get used to performing rituals and ceremonies. You may feel embarrassed and self-conscious and you will have to get used to moving about in clothes to which you are unaccustomed. But remember that there are no fears you cannot master or overcome yourself so long as you really strive and act in a reasonable manner. It is a steep learning curve but one that reaps rewards.

RECORD KEEPING

It is a good idea to write a brief entry about the ritual in your Book of Illumination (a personal record of spells, poems and other useful information). Include time and place, who was there and the purpose, so that as time passes you can look back and see what you have achieved.

△ At the start of every working, it is essential to focus on its purpose.

△ Candles should be snuffed or pinched out completely to signify that the work is done.

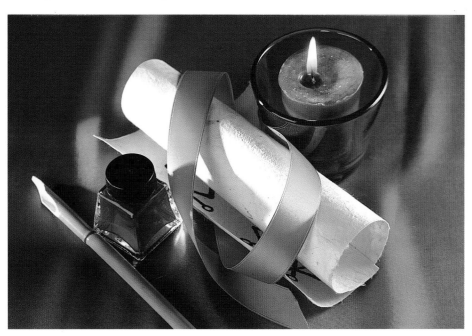

△ Talismans may be made and blessed during a ritual.

The Four Directions, the Four Guardians and

the Four Elements

When you are performing a ritual it is helpful to work with, amongst other things, the four directions of the compass, four guardians and the four elements. These will form a basis for you to begin your ritual as you construct your circle by representing the four Elements at the North, South, East and West, and then inviting the guardians to these points. They will also protect your magic circle and help you in your work.

The Four Directions

Although magic is worked in a circle almost universally, the four points of the compass are often marked in some way. In ceremonial magic where there are often a number of people working in a lodge, there may be an officer for each Element seated at the four quarters, and each of these people may have a small altar beside them on which a cloth of the relevant colour is placed and perhaps the four magical instruments of the ceremonial

△ **The Angel Gabriel is called upon to protect the magic circle.**

magician, the Pentacle in the North, the Chalice in the West, the Sword in the South, and the Wand in the East.

The Four Guardians

At the opening of the ritual it is usual to welcome the guardians of the four quarters. Every tradition has its own set of these – for example Qabalists often have the four Archangels: Raphael, whose name means "Healer of God" in the East; Michael, the Angel who is "Like unto God" in the South; Gabriel, the "Strength of God" in the West; and Auriel or Uriel, "Light of God" in the North. These angels may be seen as tall human-like figures with wings, standing guard at the four quarters. Their names are pronounced in separate syllables, for example Michael is said as Mik-I-el, not as the name, Michael, and the "el' part of any angelic name is "God". Each angel is a messenger of God with special powers, and a dictionary of Angels will explain all of their names and symbols and specialities as far as humans are concerned.

Often at the opening of a ritual the Arch-angels are described out loud, to facilitate a clearly imagined image. Raphael is robed in the colours of Air, pale blues and white of the sky, or the yellows and peaches of sunrise. Michael is dressed in scarlet and gold armour and he carries a sword with a flame-shaped blade. Gabriel carries a great chalice or Grail and wears silver, blues and sea-green as he is an Angel of Water, and Uriel, as an Earth Angel, has the colours of the seasons – black, brown, green and the gold of ripe corn. There are some wonderful pre-Raphaelite paintings of Angels which could be used as symbols on the altars if you would like to use them.

△ **The Lady of the Lake symbolizes Otherworldly power and guidance.**

The Arthurian Guardians

If you work with the tradition of the Holy Grail, you might like to have four of the main characters of the legends as keepers of the quarters. For example, King Arthur could be in the East as the master of the mysteries. Imagine a crowned king seated on a great white horse with his battle banner flying overhead with its red dragon. In his hand is a tall spear or lance, its point tipped with blood-red light, and his cloak is blown out behind him as he faces into the rising sun. Feel this as a moment of anticipation, just before the action begins.

In the South you could have the Queen's champion, Gawain, whose name means "Hawk of May", dressed in chain mail with a sword and shield, on which is painted a green pentagram on a white background. He is the defender of all that is right, a man of action and intent.

In the West you could have the Lady of the Lake, a pagan priestess or sorceress who keeps the ancient mysteries and guards their secrets. She holds the Holy Grail on her lap as she sits on a throne, carved like a boat's prow, with water flowers and creatures. She is the mistress of wisdom and the far-seer, a dreamer and visionary.

To the North you could have Merlin, the Arch Mage of Britain, wearing a hooded cloak of dark blue, studded with stars which glitter in the twilight. He holds a stone or glass ball through which he can command the destinies of humanity.

Although his face is shadowed, you know his eyes are kind and full of compassion, for he is the master of magics and will teach all who are daring enough to learn. You may find him in a cave, or in a tower surrounded by flowering hawthorn.

Greeting the Guardians

Each of these Archangels or Arthurian guardians should be treated with respect, like honoured guests.

They will come and surround your circle with protection, light and power if you are open to perceiving them with inner eyes.

You can't command them, as they are far older, bigger and more powerful than you are, but they will assist you if invited, and will fade from your perception at the end of the ritual. If you aren't able to accept them as separate beings, you can see them as parts of your own inner self, or as archetypes derived from the collective unconscious.

△ **Michael is the archangel usually depicted with a sword and a pair of scales. His direction is the South.**

SPELL TO SEE YOUR GUARDIAN ANGEL

Try this simple exercise in creative visualization to see your own angel.

1 Set out a chair and a lighted white candle on a small table, with sweet incense burning. A picture of an Angel may help too. Sing "Angel fair, angel bright, fill my life with your light." Watch the candle flame.

2 Imagine a long ladder reaching up to the sky and see an angel coming down it towards you. Sing the rhyme again, see the angel stand before you. Sing the spell again and feel the power flowing over you.

3 Sing "Angel coming from above, I thank you deeply with my love." The Angel will fade away when it has blessed you.

Earth
A vineyard symbolizes Earth's rich harvest.

Water
Crashing waves show the power of Water.

Fire
A volcano is a gift from the planet's heart.

Air
Moving clouds demonstrate Air's motion.

THE FOUR ELEMENTS

The other important matters to consider include the four Elements of Earth, Water, Fire and Air, for it is from the balance between these forces, both as symbols and within each individual, that the strength to handle the vast powers of magic can be developed.

The Communion

Many ceremonies involve a magical feast or communion, and for these you will need consumable versions of the four Elements. You will need a chalice or beautiful goblet for the wine. You will also need a platter for the bread or other sacred food. Sharing bread and wine is a part of a very ancient love-feast, called by the Greeks an Agape, which links humans with the gods of their tradition. The bread represents the nourishment of the Earth, who feeds and sustains us, and the wine the spirit of the God of the vine which uplifts us. Fire and Air may also be shared by warming your hands over the candle or lamp and by smelling the incense or scented flowers. In some workings, a scented flower, such as a rose or lily, is placed on the altar so that its perfume may be attributed to Air.

Naming, wedding and divorcing

Rites of Passage

As people pass through their lives the societies they live in may have ways of marking the passage of time, and holding celebrations to mark these phases. Most religions have a way of naming a baby and accepting it into their faith. Others have rites at puberty or first menses; among some traditional peoples this could take the form of painful initiations for the youngsters, who were then judged to be adults within their community. So-called civilized modern society no longer has real coming-of-age marking points in many religions. This can be seen as an explanation for some of today's youth trying to behave in a more grown up manner than is appropriate.

Naming Ceremonies

Within the blossoming pagan religions, new ceremonies are being constructed which can be offered to adherents, so that their children can be named and blessed in the power of the old Gods and Goddesses, without the child being committed to that religion at a very young age. Historically, one of the tasks of the village midwife was to bless a baby at its birth, before the priest of the orthodox religion named it. Today there are pagan priestesses trained in these arts and their skills are much in demand.

Coming-of-age Rituals

Rituals are being set up so that young people can be seen to have passed into adulthood, and they are given the symbols of the responsibilities they are taking on. These rituals are different from those of earlier traditions that might have involved a hunting ritual for boys, or a time apart for girls, but they can be part teaching session and part celebration. In a magical community, at the chosen age in years, or moment in life, a ritual is organized where the young person is presented with their own magical tools, their Tarot pack or symbol of the clan or community. They will be told of their responsibilities, which may increase if they are initiated into the Mysteries of their family, and they are shown the kind of assistance and support that is available to them within the community. In most magical and witch groups young people do not receive full initiation until they are 18 years old, and in some groups the starting age is as late as 21.

△ **Marriage ceremonies all over the world involve elaborate preparations.**

Wedding Rituals

There have always been ways of uniting couples in marriage, even if such ways are not recognized by the state. Weddings over the broomstick, or hand-fastings, have taken place in many parts of the world, in which the couple step over a besom to indicate they are entering a new phase of a shared

TRADITIONS OF MARRIAGE

A ring, as a symbol of the unbroken circle of lives, having no beginning or end, is an excellent way of showing the commitment to each other for a long time.

The bouquet of flowers is the last vestige of the old sacrifice which once would have been some animal or bird, offered on the altar and becoming part of the wedding feast. Even now, brides cast their bouquet over their shoulder so that another person can catch it and expect to be the next to be wed.

The parties at the Stag Night for the groom and the Hen Night or Bride Shower for the bride may have evolved from the competitive games that were held in some ancient societies. Often, the bride had to be "stolen" from her family and taken into the groom's family house or community, and there might have been a chase.

The groom would swoop into the bride's territory on a horse and carry her off to a new life, chased by her family and his friends.

life. Often a ritual is led by a pagan priest, or the matriarch or patriarch among the gypsy families who have retained these traditions. The bride and groom have their hands bound together with a ribbon, and there is an exchange of rings.

Today in pagan circles, although a priestess and priest will officiate, the actual marriage is always between the couple, allowing them to promise to love, support and remain with each other for a traditional "year and a day", or a lifetime or forever. They usually have a pair of wedding rings blessed by the priestess and priest, and exchange these as a sign of long-term commitment. There is often a ceremonial sharing of bread and wine, and often the glass is broken by the bride and groom to show that no one else can break their union. Many pagans like to conduct these marriage rites out of doors, in a sacred circle, ringed by lighted candles, flowers and ribbons. Their guests are instructed as to what may happen, as they may be from many faiths, perhaps being asked to light a candle of their own, to offer gifts or to speak personal blessings and wishes for the future of the couple. There is a feast, a cake and a party afterwards in many cases.

△ **Pagans have a ceremony called "hand fasting", equivalent to a wedding ceremony.**

△ **Horseshoes have long been used to bring luck at weddings or nailed over house doors to ensure harmony and health dwells within**.

Divorce Rituals

Although people promise to devote themselves to each other for life in the modern world, some of the unions don't stand the test of time, or the couple grow away from each other. In the past, people struggled to make a marriage last, trying to hide their differences or find ways of respecting them and continuing their lives together. Now people are more ready to split up if they have grown apart.

For this reason, rituals of division have been created which try to signify an ending that is peaceful and not acrimonious. Usually the couple are led by some members of the

pagan priesthood to acknowledge that they cannot reconcile their differences, have fallen out of love, and desire to part. Here the rings are taken off, and possibly thrown into running water, or given to a goldsmith who can melt them down, undoing the magic of joining. A ribbon that has been tied around the couple is cut and they are set free, perhaps by burning a paper on which their original bonds were written. A cake may be symbolically cut in half, or some other indication of the parting is shown to those assembled to help at this difficult time.

Choosing Your Own Ritual

The most important part of this kind of ceremony is that it is the true will – that is the considered beliefs and wishes – of the two

SEVERING THE TIES

When relationships are no longer able to sustain themselves, a symbolic ritual is sometimes called for which severs the ties that have bound the pair together, and helps to heal any bitterness or uncertainty.

In earlier times, the partners' names were written on a log of wood which was split, and each part burned on one of the ex-partners' fires to release any lingering bonds.

people involved that is paramount, rather than imposing upon them a fixed set of dogma and procedures. As far as possible the couple themselves would have dictated the form, words, setting and promises of their wedding, and in the same way, should they separate, the terms, symbols and conditions have to be for the best of all concerned. Should they part acrimoniously and only one partner be there to sever the links which they forged together, a slightly different approach is used, but many of the same symbols of cutting free or breaking the bonds are used. Perhaps the cut ribbon would be sent to the other partner to show that the relationship has been ended, but it should be done as gently as possible, as anger incurs more bad karma and will cause more problems.

Coming of age, initiation, rebirth and death –

Rites of Passage

Rites of passage are common to all societies. One that is important to all those practising witchcraft and magic is the initiation into their art. Another rite that is performed by those both inside and outside the world of magic is the one to mark someone's passing on from this life: the funeral. We will also look at the belief held by many occultists, that of rebirth. In between these is the rite of coming of age.

Coming of Age

Entering into adulthood is a time when those who wish to enter one of the pagan paths can receive initiation, although many of today's candidates are somewhat older. Taking on magical power, whether as a witch, druid or a ritual magician, is a heavy burden and the newcomer needs to understand life before being ready for the work. Some kinds of wisdom do come with age, and the occult world has tended to realize this.

Initiation and Rebirth

A magical initiation has many of the same symbols as a traditional coming-of-age ceremony would have had in simpler societies. The candidate is faced with a challenge. She or he may have been taught what to expect, or in today's world, where information is readily available, may have been able to read up on the ritual, or talked to those who had gone through it. However, it will always throw up some surprises, on both practical and physical levels. There may be a time of darkness when the candidate is blindfold in the presence of strangers. She or he may be dressed in an unfamiliar way, lightly bound with a guiding rope, and important words will be spoken to the candidate.

The candidate may be asked to make a promise of secrecy, respect for their fellows, and honour to the tradition being entered, and take a new name, which itself may be secret. Eventually the inner matters of the group, lodge or coven will be shown to the candidate as symbols, tools or information. Then she or he will be welcomed into the community as an equal and honoured participant.

Some ritual initiations include a death and rebirth enactment, showing that the neophyte (literally new-born) member is now part of a different family. But it is also expressing the belief that people live many lives, that they are reborn, after a time of reassessment and rest, into the same world they left at death. It is part of many initiates' training that they understand this transition by meditating on death and the afterlife, on reincarnation and rebirth, planning for what may happen.

REMEMBRANCE SHRINE

When someone has died the ones who are left to grieve find comfort in marking a particular place in the house where they can go to remember and celebrate a life that has moved on. A remembrance shrine can be made from photographs, a lit candle, some burning incense, some fresh flowers or a keepsake that reminds you of that person. Make this a shrine of affirmation of a life rather than continual mourning for a loss.

△ **Death is but a short step through the gates of the otherworld, from which we return reborn.**

Funerals

Of course, the passing of a friend and magical colleague is a great sadness to those left behind, but pagan funerals tend to be celebrations of the life that has been, rather than gloomy and sad ceremonies held in orthodox places of worship. Pagans may be buried, many preferring a woodland burial in a biodegradable coffin and a living tree planted, rather than a dead headstone as a memorial. Others are cremated so that their ashes may be ritually scattered at some sacred or beloved spot by their friends.

Sometimes the ceremony, carried out at a crematorium, which is multi-faith in its approach these days, will allow for a magical circle to be cast about the coffin, floral tributes in the shapes of stars or circles, and readings of ritual prayers or poetry. Symbolic acts of casting off the mortal life for the eternal spiritual one can be shared by the family and friends, anecdotes of the deceased's life, even photographs of them at different stages can be shared. Joy should be felt as well as sorrow.

The Life Cycle

Because witches and magicians see the Earth as a Great Mother Goddess, the burial or scattering of ashes is returning the physical remains to the place from which it was born and so completing a cycle. We have to acknowledge that we are all created of the substance of the Earth through the food we eat and the air we breathe, but this Earth is part of the initial impulse in the first moment of creation. So are all the stars, the suns and planets, and we are also part of this first coming into being too, eternal, ever changing but immortal.

A FUNERAL POEM

Many people find the following poem comforting, be they followers of pagan or orthodox faiths.

Do not stand at my grave and weep,
I am not there, I do not sleep.
I am a thousand winds that blow,
I am the diamond glints on snow,
I am the sunlight on ripened grain,
I am the gentle autumn rain.
When you wake from sleep in the
　morning's hush,
I am the swift, uplifting rush
Of quiet birds in circling flight.
I am the soft starlight at night.
Do not stand at my grave and cry,
I am not there, I did not die.

A version of a poem written by an anonymous soldier in Northern Ireland.

△ **Burials among great trees are becoming popular among pagans or humanists.**

Rebirth

After death, it is considered by many occultists, that the soul is drawn towards a great light. People who have clinically died and been brought back to life in hospitals often describe passing through a dark tunnel towards a place of brightness, and perhaps encountering an Angel, a Christ figure or dead relative who may lead them to a glorious garden. Somehow they then sense an undeniable call back to earth, and return to complete their life, usually as changed people. In this place of light or paradise garden souls may rest and, with the guidance of their guardian Angels, assess their past life, seeing it dispassionately. After this, there is a timeless eon of rest, before the process of preparing for rebirth into the world begins. Some believe that we choose our parents and the kind of social position, health and conditions ourselves to maximize our personal evolution.

Those who have evolved through many thousands of lives and, according to the Buddhist belief, have been able to step off the wheel of incarnations, may still choose to return to Earth, to teach others, or act as a beacon, guiding lost souls towards their heavenly or divine heritage. Some people seem to return quickly to a new life, especially if they have died in a war or accident and been cut off from completing their allotted span. Others return only after long intervals of Earthly time.

Affirm the life you are living now and keep mementos and reminders of the days that are passing. Childhood is a fleeting phase, and should be marked and recorded with reverence and joy. A book of your children's first steps and development is one way of celebrating life as it happens.

△ **Some people believe that after life we go to an island, be it Avalon or Tir na Nog, before returning.**

Working alone or together in

Covens and Lodges

Essentially, the powers of magic are shaped by each individual but most people prefer to work with others, either within a coven or group of witches, or in a magical lodge. The problem with these kinds of associations is that they have traditionally always been secret. Most magical and witchcraft groups are independent and, although there are some national and international federations which you may join, they don't necessarily point you straight to a group in your area. One way of discovering what exists will be to read the announcements in popular occult magazines. These may mention either public meetings or celebrations of festivals open to all, they may list societies or training schools, and they may list other, smaller journals that are written by specialists in the area of magic which most interests you. It has never been an easy path to find a way into the Mysteries, but these basic steps are open to all.

Covens

Followers of wicca, the more modern, revitalized form of witchcraft, usually belong to a coven, led by a High Priestess and a High Priest. Covens are small groups of both men and women, usually not exceeding 13 members, but now there are same-sex groups, and much larger gatherings of wiccans. To belong to a coven requires admittance by an initiation ritual once a candidate has been approved by the existing members. In some groups the candidate has to ask for admission, and in others a suitable person will be invited to join. Some covens have an "Outer Court", which is for non-initiates, where they may meet regularly to receive training and get to know each other.

INSIDE OR OUTSIDE

Some covens meet out of doors, in woods or high hills, in all weathers. These outdoor witches use what is around them for their symbols: water in a sea shell from rain or a spring, a small bonfire, a tree branch for a wand and their hand for a sword. Then there are the wiccans who prefer to gather inside a house. Witches may perform rituals "skyclad", naked, if they follow the works of Gerald Gardner and his successors, or wearing simple robes or tunics. Indoors, they lay out elegant altars with Goddess and God statues, candles, daggers called "athames", cords and swords, chalices and pentacles.

Recording Rituals

Many of the wiccan rituals have been written down because since the 1950s there has been in existence a "Book of Shadows" in which the words and movements of esbats, the patterns of festivals or sabbats, the initiations and degree ceremonies, spells and incantations are recorded. This used to have to be copied by hand by each new initiate, but since the advent of photocopiers and now computers, often it is a "Disc of Shadows" passed from one member to another and frequently updated.

△ **In medieval times, there were orders of initiates whose rituals were performed in chapels.**

Country Witches

The country witches of today seldom write anything down, relying – as did their predecessors – on memory and inspiration for their workings, which are usually conducted in a sacred place. Their knowledge is passed on in the old way, by apprenticeship, whereby the newcomer is gradually taught the rituals, the healing spells, the chants and the movements. They may have a way of welcoming a candidate into their circle, but their initiation is between the Gods and Goddesses of the land and the newcomer, rather than power being passed on by a High Priestess or High Priest.

△ **It is thought that powerful ceremonies were carried out in ancient times within Stonehenge.**

Ritual Occasions

Most witches and wiccans hold gatherings at the full Moon, as well as at a number of festivals each year. As well as celebrating the season, work may be done to divine the future, to discuss the admittance of new members, or to work on some longer term ecological problem, for example. Some rituals are used to raise the wiccan from one degree to the next, in a similar way that Freemasons are elevated through three degrees. There are quite a few links between the work of the old craft guilds of stonemasons or Foresters and modern wicca.

Lodges

Ritual magicians meet in lodges, which are often the working groups within a school. Although the numbers of professed witches have risen enormously in the last few years, the number of ceremonial magicians has always been much smaller. Although both kinds of occult workers use similar symbols, the four Elements and may celebrate seasonal festivals, ritual magicians have a vast store of theoretical knowledge to grasp. There are a number of different traditions within Western ritual. One is the Qabalah, originally an esoteric branch of Judaism, with a glyph called the Tree of Life and a complex philosophy of magical work. Another is the Seekers of the Holy Grail, a mysterious object that will bring healing and harmony if it can be restored to its rightful place. Here the main theme of magical work is based around the personal quest, and knowledge is gained as the seeker journeys through the inner realms of magic. Many of the classical religions have a magical side, and the Northern Runic and Celtic traditions have

△ Some groups of practical magicians hold their rituals out of doors at ancient sacred sites.

left a heritage of ritual, symbolism and legend that attracts followers today.

Ceremonial Magic

This has a single school, while others are derived from more recent developments of ancient wisdom. One of the most influential was the Hermetic Order of the Golden Dawn, founded in London, England, in 1887 by a number of Freemasons. They had come upon a body of practical magic based upon several ancient sources, which set out a curriculum of training, a series of initiations and grade rituals, and a vast collection of information on astrology, talismans, ceremonial equipment and the Tarot. Many of the modern Tarot packs draw on the symbolism, interpretation and images developed by members of the Golden Dawn Order at the start of the 20th century. There were

originally four lodges, in London; Weston-super-Mare, Somerset; Bradford, Yorkshire; and Edinburgh, Scotland.

The main organization began to break up, so one of the members, F. Israel Regardie published the material in the 1930s, breaking his oath of secrecy as he felt that this was such a valuable magical source that it should be available to a wider readership.

The Golden Dawn is still functioning worldwide. As the books are still in print new generations of students can use them for guidance and inspiration. The Golden Dawn drew on many sources of esoteric knowledge, including the earlier Rosicrucian tradition and the Hermetic Mysteries of ancient Egypt. Magic has changed little in this long heritage, and it has given strength and endurance to those who work with it today.

SPELL TO FIND A MAGICAL TEACHER OR PATH
Magic is best taught by a living person but you might need some help from other sources in finding one. Try this spell if you are looking for help and guidance.

1 During a waning Moon, light a blue candle and place it beside the thickest magical book you possess.

2 Concentrate on your need, writing it on a new sheet of paper in black ink. Fold this into a narrow bookmark shape. Say out loud "I desire to find a path/teacher to lead me, on the road to magic. In this book I seek; in this book I peek. Reveal a clue, now heed me."

3 Slide the strip of paper into the book at random and quickly read the words next to the paper. This will help your quest if your intent is clear. Pinch out the candle.

△ The Knights Templar were an order of crusading Christians who preserved ancient secrets.

Initiation, commitment, responsibility are the
Ethics of Witchcraft

Because workers of magic and witches do not belong to orthodox religions, many people imagine that they either have no moral rules or that they worship evil. The truth of this matter is that they are very strongly ethical in their work because they realize that, working with powerful forces for change, they have to ensure that those changes are for the better. It is often stated that the witches Rune contains a very positive ethic. It states "If you harm none, do what you will." On the face of it, it looks like a licence to do anything, but it means "so long as you cause no harm to any person, animal or thing, you may follow your True Will." True Will is not a personal choice or want, but the purpose of your existence on Earth; the reason you are alive is to discover this and work towards it. If you cause harm to anyone, that harm will be reflected back on you, if not in this life then in another incarnation, there is no escape. However, if you do good, then that too is reflected back to you.

△ **Formal initiation rituals involving three degrees are shared by Freemasons and wiccans.**

Beliefs

Magicians do not believe the stories in the Bible about God having an adversary called Satan. That is part of the orthodox religion and it is not part of paganism. Pagans believe that there are two forces: one is called Cosmos and strives towards order and wholeness; the other is called Chaos and tends towards dissolution and re-formation. Both are positive forces; one constructing, the other breaking down through change. If the second force did not exist, nothing that died would ever decay, and no transformations could occur from fallen leaves into compost and

into strong new growth. These forces need to balance and be in harmony. Evil is what people consciously or unconsciously do in the world, there is no being or energy which is of itself evil.

Initiation

Many of those who are involved in magic and witchcraft undergo a ceremony of admission to their tradition that is called initiation. This is a serious and enduring step to take and usually groups train their novices before guiding them to, and then through, the initiation ritual. Each tradition has its own symbols and deity names, which are shown to the initiate at that time, and though details of some of these ceremonies have been published, the actual experience of going through them is emotional and significant, and in some cases life-altering.

The word "initiation" means "to enter in", so it is a first step, rather than the conclusion of a magician's work, but no one should accept initiation into any group unless they are certain that it is right for them, and that the group is trustworthy. If there are any doubts in a novice's mind it is far better to wait than to rush into a situation. Another, better, chance will occur when the time and circumstances are right.

△ **Large gatherings of magical orders, such as the Knights Templar, are no longer common.**

GETTING USED TO PERFORMING RITUALS

△ Those undergoing initiation into any Mystery group might encounter strange visions.

There are no vengeful Gods lurking unseen, but there are inner depths within you that can be challenged and unravelled, or that can make their presence known like a rotting carcass under your nose. If you have seriously tried to improve your human character, and have striven to raise yourself up, nothing can or will harm you. There are no fears that you cannot master or overcome by yourself so long as you are really trying to learn and are acting in a reasonable manner. Certainly it will feel very strange the first few times you dress up and perform your rituals. You may feel embarrassed and self-conscious, even if you are alone. You will have to get used to moving about in a long skirt and dealing effectively with all the regalia of ritual; you will need to learn to cope with a strange state of consciousness, yet move and walk, talk and think while partly in this world and partly out of it.

Hierarchies

Some organizations in ceremonial magic and wicca have several degrees or further initiations, which again should not be rushed into. Claiming to hold some high office means very little if you don't have the knowledge and experience to handle the forces effectively or work with the God forms of that level. Usually those who talk most about their position and grade are the least worthy. As the Bible says, "Empty vessels make the most noise."

Each individual lodge has a number of officers, both male and female, whose positions have traditionally reflected their state on the ladder of initiation. Some represent the forces of the Elements others act as guardians of the heritage, or teachers who reveal the secrets to each generation. There are basic rituals for opening the lodge, for creating a sacred space within the working temple, summoning the powers who protect and energize each working, and initiating new members or advancing those qualified. It is a very structured system and may seem rather old fashioned today.

However, the wisdom within this tradition has gradually been reshaped to suit a more egalitarian community, and though modern magicians draw on the material, they may not necessarily be bound by all its strictures.

△ Dionysus, the god of the vine, is called to initiate the candidate into his mystery.

Commitment and Secrecy

Although we now live in a far more open society than that of old, it is still best to keep some things secret and go about your magical work in privacy and silence, both of which add to the power. There are a few things that are never spoken of by effective magicians. These include who is working magic, when and where any magic or ritual is being done (unless it is some sort of public festival) and any magical names and mottos used. These are only ever known to the magicians and the Gods. You can read books on most techniques or activities, but it is the practical experience of magic that makes it work, and that is a particular secret that cannot be shared.

If you meddle in the affairs of others who did not ask for help, you will reap the harvest you have sown. If you have any uncontrolled psychic abilities, you can end up having unpleasant experiences, drawn from unexplored aspects of your own nature. Losing the ability to meditate or be calm is sufficient to show that you have transgressed the code of magical ethics.

By the Light of the Sun, Moon and Stars

From the earliest times we have watched the sky, observing the path of the Sun, the changing face of the Moon and the movements of the planets and stars. From these come stories of Gods and Goddesses, and a rich heritage of myth and magic.

The Moon

Its Cycles, Rituals and Magic

All life on Earth is governed by cycles. Some are quite short, for example day and night, and others are quite long, such as the solar year. Each cycle has its use in magic, and every time and season has benefits and strengths that can be used to gain insights, to develop skills and assist the magicians to grow in wisdom. It is by learning to be in phase with the natural cycles rather than struggling against the tides of the world that our paths become smoother and our magic more effective.

△ **The Moon is seen as female and is often personified as a beautiful goddess.**

The Cycle of the Moon

It is important to understand the changes of the Moon, and why she waxes and wanes each month, for her power is used in magic. Her light can guide the lost in midnight's darkness. She also reflects the changing nature of women and, just as she rules the sea, she affects the body, which contains a great deal of water. The Moon actually alters the moods of many people, bringing periods of lucid dreams, visions or greater psychic sensitivity.

You can imagine the three separate Goddesses – the Maid, Mother and the Matriarch – each teaching you things; or just see her as a barren globe, circling our home planet. If you imagine a dark night with the sky lit by many stars, and then allow whichever phase of the moon you wish to work with to flood that darkness with silvery light, you will begin to sense her effect upon you.

The Moon and Dreams

Once you start to observe the phases of the Moon and her movements in the sky, which are far less predictable than those of the sun, you may begin to notice the phases in your own life. There are natural peaks and troughs of energy, feelings and inspiration or creativity, and to some extent these may be reflected in the way you dream. If you get enough sleep, which really is important for your physical and psychic health, you should start to record the sorts of dreams you have when you wake each day. At first they may just drift away, but if you tell your subconscious mind to recall your dreams, just before you go to sleep, you will find memories start to remain.

Working with the Moon's Cycle

Many of the mental arts of magic are similar to inducing dreams to happen when you are awake, so the clearer the communication between your inner and outer mind at night, the brighter will be the visions seen when you scry (divine by crystal-gazing) or meditate. Because the Moon's phases affect dreaming cycles in most people, this can be used to enhance the power of magic. You can work a spell to bring about finding a new job, for example, and then dream of finding yourself in the sort of place you would like to work, or even meeting a friend who tells you about the kind of position you are seeking. Then, in real life, you find the dream being played out before you. That is how effective magic shows itself. Teach yourself to understand how the positions of the Earth and the Sun cause the Moon to

wax and wane, and change her rising and setting place and time throughout her cycles – which are actually 18 or 19 years long – before the Earth, Moon and Sun return to their starting places. Find out how she affects your moods, and find out how she affects the tides of the sea. The tides of the Moon, when her light grows or shrinks, give impetus to the sort of magic you might wish to do.

△ **The Moon rules the tides of the sea.**

A MOON RITUAL

Here is a simple Moon ritual which can be tried to request help. A good time is around the full Moon. Decide which of your activities requires light or encouragement and, in the evening, when the Moon has risen, set out an altar with white and silver items, three candles, a silver or glass bowl of spring water, a new piece of white paper, an envelope, and a black or silver pen. Prepare yourself by dressing for the ritual, and light an aromatherapy burner with some jasmine or lavender oil.

2 Seal the envelope carefully. Hold it below each candle so that the light of the candle shines on it. Don't let the paper singe or burn.

1 Light the three candles from left to right, saying "Moon Maiden, inspire me, Moon Mother protect me, and Moon Matriarch empower me, as I ask this favour. At this hour of bright moonlight, please help me to shine at the work I do" (or other matter you are requesting help with). Pause for a few moments, really focusing on your spell, and then write your exact and precise need.

3 Then sprinkle the envelope with water, saying, "Maiden bless me, Mother guide me, and Matriarch assist me that my will be done." Hide the envelope and see what happens by the next full Moon. You will be surprised at the results.

The Three Faces of the Moon

Using Moon magic often involves three candles, which may be white or silver, or perhaps the colours associated with the Maid, Mother and Matriarch, which are white, red and black or dark blue. These three Goddesses align to the phases of the Moon:

1 The Maiden, who is everyone's daughter, playmate and inspirer is the new moon.

2 The Mother, who guides our lives, teaches us the skill of living, and heals us, is our mystical lover at full Moon.

3 The Matriarch or Crone, who gives wisdom, magical knowledge and the power to see into the future is the Moon as she wanes into darkness.

Everyone can call upon the help these Goddesses offer, perhaps naming them from a pantheon. The Greeks called upon Artemis the huntress with her silver bow, protector of animals and children, the spotless maiden. They called upon golden Aphrodite as the goddess of love and beauty, born of the foam of the sea, the all mother, to help them. They worshipped Hecate, dark goddess of the underworld, honoured at crossroads, who teaches magic and ancient wisdom when the sky is dark. The Romans built temples dedicated to Diana, and to Luna, and to many of the light-bringers. The Ancient Egyptians had a moon God, Thoth, rather than a goddess, and in England we talk about the man in the moon.

△ Stars are seen as symbols of life and hope and, with Suns and Moons are used in magic.

△ Hecate is the goddess of crossroads, owls and nightmares, but offers wisdom to the daring.

The Sun

Its Healing Power and Rituals

Throughout classical mythology, the Sun was seen as a symbol of the Gods and Goddesses and was worshipped for its healing powers. Magicians and witches take the light of the Sun into account when they are working magic. As you become more aware of it, you will notice how it affects your life, your dreams and your magic. The Sun is often seen as a representative of the individual in his or her world, the light radiating is the way he or she is seen by friends and family. If someone is ill, it is as if the light of their personal Sun is dimmed and so spells are sung which encourage the light to shine.

△ **The Greek Sun god, Helios or Apollo, drives the quadriga, the Chariot of the Sun.**

△ **Ancient stone circles have an inextricable relationship with the sun.**

The Sun

The power of the Sun is concerned with life – we wouldn't exist if it were not for the precise interaction of Sun and Earth, heat and radiation, gravity and distance, that ensure the dynamic balance of our solar system. But this is a delicate balance, and is not immutable. The light of the Sun is necessary for health, and generally makes us feel brighter, happier and well, but too much can be harmful.

Sun Legends

The Sun God is traditionally born at the dead of winter soon after the solstice. He grows with each passing day, and receives his sword and arrows from his Mother, the ever-virgin Earth Goddess. Later, as the year turns, he becomes her lover. At midsummer he is at his height and yet, to feed the people, as the corn king, he has to be cut down at harvest. The Earth Goddess receives him and takes him into her house. This is still symbolized by the corn dolly, made from the last sheaf of standing corn.

These legends form part of the ritual pattern of many of the modern covens of witches, with the high priest and priestess acting out the story of the God and Goddess. The Druids follow this cycle, and many other pagans also work their way through the stories of the old Gods.

Autumn brings the bonfires of Hallowe'en, Summer's End. Traditionally, on this ghostly eve, all the dead return to join the revels, and unborn children meet their parents in spirit. As the king of winter, the God at his lowest ebb rules with his queen, Lady of Night, and at midwinter he is born again, the star child, the bringer of hope in darkness.

△ **Ra, Lord of the Horizon, represents the Sun at dawn.**

The Healing Power of the Sun

To use the Sun directly as a healing force requires little in the way of equipment or preparation. If you are unwell, merely sitting relaxed in a sunny spot, and imagining the light from the sky shining through you in brilliant white-gold rays, driving out the darkness of disease, bringing relief from pain or stiffness, can be sufficient to get your own inner-healing processes going.

If you have a sick friend, tell them to do the same. As they sit calmly in a sunny place, explain to them how the vitalizing beams of light can help to set off the healing process and drive out infection. This technique uses relaxation, which is very important in every kind of healing, and the imagination, to overcome and drive out the illness.

△ **The sun offers a healing power all of its own.**

A Guide to Healthy Living

Include raw fruits and vegetables in your diet and choose organically-grown produce and naturally-reared meat as well as free-range eggs. The blessing of Nature and the light of the Sun will enrich your diet. Don't add salt or sugar or any processed flavourings to your food but rely on herbs and spices to flavour both raw and cooked foods. Keep an eye on your weight without being obsessed with dieting and you will lessen your chances of being afflicted with many complaints. Include a little exercise in your week, such as walking, dancing, swimming, riding, cycling or aerobic movements. Devote some time to meditation, relaxation, creative visualization or a similar activity, and you ought to be able to live a healthy life.

A SUN RITUAL

You may decide that you would like to bring more light into your life by aligning yourself with the solar power, especially at a time like the Spring Equinox or Midsummer. You could use these times of year to make a personal dedication to following the path of light. To do this you would need to prepare a short ritual in which you promise, as long as the Sun rises in the morning and sets at night, to strive towards magical skills, or to be a healer, to create a garden, or help your community or a local nature reserve. Whatever you choose to promise has to be within your capabilities.

On a Sunday or sunny day set out an altar covered in gold or yellow with two gold or yellow candles, a piece of paper, a pen that writes gold, matches, a heatproof container, a cup of golden fruit juice and a round biscuit. Bathe or shower and put on your robe if you have one, or clean clothes, including something yellow or gold if possible. Make sure you have everything you need, including charcoal if you are burning incense, perhaps some yellow or golden flowers, and any symbols of the Sun you may have, including brass or a gold ornament.

Before you begin, walk round in a circle sunwise, asking for protection, for strength and for enlightenment. When you have finished, realize that your promise is real and will endure. In the next month you will discover clues as to how it will work out.

1 Light one candle to represent yourself, and the other to represent the Sun. Sit down and meditate for a while on how the Sun influences your life, and how you in turn influence others.

2 Write your Sun promise as clearly and accurately as you can on the piece of paper. You may also like to state your promise aloud.

3 Carefully light the paper in one of the candle flames, so in essence it is taken up to the Sun. Drop the burning paper into a heatproof container and reflect on what you have done.

4 Bless and eat the biscuit, then the drink, in the name of a Sun deity. Snuff the candles and unwind the circle widdershins.

Working with the
Signs of the Zodiac

The art of astrology is very ancient and is based on the constellations which appear in a wide band around the Earth. In most ancient systems there were 12 signs:

1   Aries the Ram
2   Taurus the Bull
3   Gemini the Twins
4   Cancer the Crab
5   Leo the Lion
6   Virgo the Virgin
7   Libra the Scales
8   Scorpio the Scorpion
9   Sagittarius the Archer
10 Capricorn the Sea goat
11 Aquarius the Water bearer
12 Pisces the Fishes

Originally the stars of these signs would have been seen in the sky at night and, though their light and patterns are hidden in daytime, astrologers knew where they would be found.

Many of the constellations were orginally seen as animals or mythical beasts.

The Horoscope

To construct a horoscope, an astrologer needs to know not only the time and date of a person's birth, but their exact location on the planet at birth in longitude and latitude. From these data a unique chart can be constructed showing not only the position of the Sun against the zodiac, the Sun sign, but the sign which was at that time rising over the eastern horizon, which is called the ascendant or rising sign. Because the signs move through the heavens at the rate of one sign every month, each Sun sign changes then.

Against the slow and steady movement of the zodiac around the sky the faster, apparently more erratic movements of the planets are plotted. Although we know the Sun is the true centre of our solar system, with the planets and their moons revolving in a great ellipse around that star, astrology makes the Earth the centre of the chart, and shows the positions of the other heavenly bodies from that perspective. In this way some of the planets can seem to move backwards, with what is called retrograde motion.

The Planetary Rulers

Each person's horoscope contains not only the actual position of the planets within the signs of the zodiac but the strengths of their relationships to each other.

Each sign of the zodiac has a planetary ruler, and if the planet is in its own sign then it can be an important feature in the horoscope. Included in the planets are the Sun and the Moon. Neither of these is actually a planet, the Moon being Earth's satellite, and the Sun being our nearest star, but they are treated as planets to assist interpretation of the chart.

The Configuration

Each sign of the zodiac has certain qualities and influences, as do each of the planets, and it is this individual configuration at a person's birth that shows their potential; their strengths and weaknesses.

Many people think that they only partake of the power of one sign whereas, in reality, they draw on many signs of the zodiac, including the ascendant, the positions of the major planets and other significant relationships to make them the unique person they are. An astrologer will be able to interpret a horoscope in great detail and show hidden potential, possible illness or positive or difficult times in a person's life. It is necessary to bear this in mind and not feel limited by the fact that you are Taurean or Capricorn. There is much more to astrology than that.

△ **Venus is the planet that rules both Taurus the Bull and Libra the Scales.**

Learning About the Zodiac

If you want to draw on the powers of the stars for magical work, you should add to your basic knowledge of astrology. To check the exact information of positions of the planets in relationship to the signs of the zodiac, you will need to consult a book of tables called an ephemeris. You may need to know the exact time a planet enters a sign of the zodiac, or precisely when that sign begins, and this can vary. The temporal junction between two signs is called the cusp, and people born on the same day in different years may sometimes find their birthdays in different signs. Note also that sidereal or star time differs from clock time. If you wish to follow this subject more deeply, there is plenty of information available.

△ **The traditional signs from a Singhalese manuscript link Eastern and Western astrology.**

△ **An Eastern zodiac chart with Singhalese illustrations.**

THE NATURES AND ELEMENTS OF ZODIAC SIGNS

Here is a little information about each of the zodiac signs, which are governed by one of the Elements – Air, Fire, Water or Earth. The first sign of the zodiacal year, marking the Spring Equinox, is:

Aries, March to April, ruled by Mars, Fire
Taurus, April to May, ruled by Venus, Earth
Gemini, May to June, ruled by Mercury, Air
Cancer, June to July, ruled by the Moon, Water
Leo, July to August, ruled by the Sun, Fire
Virgo, August to September, ruled by Mercury, Earth
Libra, September to October, ruled by Venus, Air
Scorpio, October to November, ruled by Pluto and Mars, Water
Sagittarius, November to December, ruled by Jupiter, Fire
Capricorn, December to January, ruled by Saturn, Earth
Aquarius, January to February, ruled by Uranus and Saturn, Air
Pisces, February to March, ruled by Neptune and Jupiter, Water

Astrology, Charms and Talismans

In magic and witchcraft, certain objects are used which act as mystical telephone numbers, summoning a specific power, be it a God, an Angel, an Elemental force or kind of luck. These mystical objects can differ for witches and for ceremonial magicians. Witches tend to use charms and these are natural objects. Ceremonial magicians, however, will make items specifically for their workings. They make these using astrological principles and with particular thought for the purpose in mind. Talismans are a means of drawing down the power of the planets into a scroll, or an object, which can then be used as a powerful magical tool.

Charms

An example of the charms used in witchcraft are stones with natural holes in them. These perforated flints or fossils are called holy or holey stones and were used to prevent harm from coming to animals. The stones were collected, often from a beach or river bank, and hung on red wool or ribbon over the doors of cattle sheds or stables. This was to stop elves coming and milking the cows, or night hags riding the horses in the

△ Each planet in our solar system is named after a God or Goddess.

hours of darkness. It was supposed that evil forces would be attracted to the holes in the stones and try to get through, and so become trapped. Traditionally, these stones were thrown into running water after seven years so that any harm trapped in them would be washed away, then new stones were found and hung up.

Other charms include herbs: mint for money if carried in the purse, sage for wisdom, oak to protect from lightning when put into a

small red cloth charm bag and worn every day. Some fossils were thought to have magical powers: belemnites were believed to be "elf shot", arrows fired by spirits to make cattle sick; and ammonites were snakes turned to stone by the magic of wizards or Christian saints. Folklore is full of these simples which were carried for protection, to bring health or luck. Charms are always some natural substance, perhaps a strange shape, such as four-leaved clovers which bring luck, and pebbles in the shape of an eye, which are thought to be protective.

Amulets

Amulets can take all shapes and will have particular relevance for the person who carries one. They are often created in the form of an eye, or made in the shape of a hand, like the Arabic Hand of Fatima, which wards off harm. An amulet has a single purpose and may be worn or carried all the time, or the form may be painted onto items such as boats to draw safe passage and good luck to those who use it.

△ Traditional holey stones, used for protection.

◁ Some talismans were richly ornamental, like this amulet made for King Charlemagne, Holy Roman Emperor from 800 to 814.

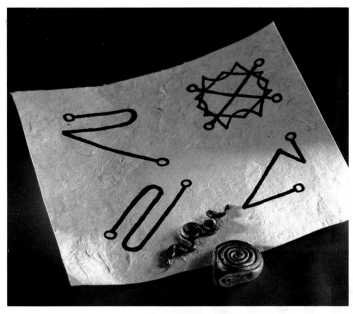
△ Talismans are still written in ancient alphabets, or use symbols that summon the help of Angels.

△ Once made and blessed, each charm is wrapped in silk, or placed in a protective pouch.

Talismans

Talismans are carefully created by the magician or witch for a particular short-term aim. They can be focused on healing a broken leg, for example, or success at a job interview. Ideally they should be made for the person whose life is intended to change. Today they might be made of coloured paper, but in the past they were sometimes made of precious metal, set with jewels, or they could be written in magical ink on parchment, or even on the hand of the sick person, or carved into

LEARNING THE NECESSARY ARTS

You may well also need to learn certain practical arts, like calligraphy, astrology, metal engraving, poker-work, embroidery or herbalism, in order that you have the necessary skill to make, consecrate and empower the talisman in a way that will ensure its success.

Many talismans are written in ancient languages, but don't use these unless you know exactly what you are doing or you might not get what you are hoping for. Some talismans are made up of numbers or symbols, some are shapes or show protective images, like the Christian St Christopher medallion which helps travellers, or the many traditional symbols or objects the world over. Black cats are lucky in Britain but it is white cats that are luck bringers in the USA, so nothing can be taken for granted.

wood or marked on soft clay and baked. The art of making talismans is extremely ancient. Some that have been found on archaeological digs in Mesopotamia seem to predate writing, and it is possible that the various alphabets developed from the symbols used to request magical help.

Using the Zodiac Signs and Planets

You will need to understand the basic powers of each zodiac sign and planet so that you can discover which one or two are most relevant to your needs. Often, two powers are used so that their colours may both be used. Each planet is associated with a number, colour, jewel, incense and symbol, and the signs of the zodiac have similar correspondences. Refer to the chart in the section "Powers of the Planets and the Days of the Week". For example, if you wanted to make yourself more assertive, this is one of the qualities of the zodiac sign Aries the Ram, whose colour is red and whose ruling planet is Mars. This would give you a base colour of scarlet, but too much assertion can become aggression, so it would be wise to temper the Martian force with that of Venus, the planet of harmony. Her colour is emerald green, her metal copper and her number seven. You could take a pentagon-shaped piece of red paper to link with Mars and write on it in green ink "I desire to be more assertive to bring harmony and strength to my life." You could do this when the Sun is in the

sign of Aries. Light seven green candles on your altar but wrap the finished talisman in red silk bound with emerald ribbon. Place it out of sight for a month.

Assembling Your Material

As well as knowing on what day and at what hour the work should be done, you will need to assemble material for the talisman, including the correct planetary metal (or something that symbolises it, like gold foil or paper), and inks to write on it. You will need a connecting link to the person for whom it is intended: hair, a signature or photograph, etc. and some silk or fine cloth of the right colour to make a cover for it. You might need clay or wood, jewels and sewing thread, felt-tip pens and parchment, metal foil and an appropriate incense.

△ The Red Planet, Mars, rules over courage, war and energy, and strengthens people born under the sign of Aries.

An effective tool

Making a Talisman

A talisman can be a very powerful and effective tool in the hands of a master or mistress of the craft. Talisman-making is a skill that is important for every witch to learn. They may be made from wax or metal or, more commonly now, from coloured paper. If you want to make a talisman you will need to establish the colour, materials, day and God forms related to the subject of your talisman, and gather such equipment as you need in order to make it. You can simply manufacture the charm and then consecrate it on your own, or you can make it magical. As you become more experienced, you will find it easier.

Creating a Talisman

Various colours or symbols can be used for different meanings and correspondences.

1 To begin you need a piece of coloured paper. Write on it with a pen that contains ink of a contrasting colour.

2 As you do this, ask yourself questions such as "Who is this talisman to be made for?" "Is it with his/her will?" "Why this shape?" "Why this colour?" "What is the purpose of the talisman?" and "By what right do I set this plan in motion?"

These questions can also be asked of you by a magical partner in a kind of shared litany. This kind of process adds enormously to the power of the completed talisman, as well as helping you to clarify your objectives.

3 If it is for yourself, link it to yourself by writing your magical name on it, signing it, or by adding a drop of your blood or saliva. Even so, it should be completed by both you and your magical partner, if you have one.

4 Finally wrap the folded piece of paper in a piece of blue silk.

△ **An ancient gnostic talisman.**

Consecrating the Talisman

When the practical part of making the talisman is complete, you then need to consecrate it. This need not be on the same day – for example, a talisman to bring success to a growing partnership, which would involve both the Sun and Venus, could be made on a Sunday and consecrated on the following Friday, or vice versa. Consecration also needs preparation. You will need some holy oil – this is usually made from almond or olive oil to which is added herbs, gums, resins or chips of wood from the incense tree dedicated to the planets concerned. This is left in the sun so that the oils and perfumes suffuse the oil. You will also need water, a lit candle, incense, charcoal, a stone, wine and bread.

1 In your magic circle, set up the temple, with the altar in the centre. Don't rush through the words or the actions as it takes time for the powers to enter the talisman.

2 Work out an invocation so that you can put into the talisman your feelings about it. You can even have another set of questions and answers which explain to the powers you are calling upon what the talisman is intended to accomplish, who it is for, and so on.

3 Sprinkle water on the talisman to cleanse it. Try not to touch the talisman afterwards. You will need to circle it with fire which, as the energizing Element, will make it come alive. If you can't pass it through a flame circle the lamp about it.

4 Now wave the talisman through the incense smoke. This will blow life into the talisman, so that it is fully effective. Sit in silent meditation for a few moments to allow any energies to spiral into the new talisman.

5 Dip your forefinger into the oil and imagine a pool of light which transfers to the talisman. Say firmly "In the Name of … I consecrate this talisman of …" and then speak your chosen invocation.

6 Wait for a surge of energy to be felt or the incense smoke to swirl or until you perceive light around the new talisman. Place the wrapped talisman under a stone to ground its power. Then share a cup of wine and bread to complete your ceremony. Do not hurry just because it seems you have completed the work.

7 When you have completed the ceremony slowly unwind the circle, put the equipment away, disrobe and come back to earth. Leave the talisman on the altar for as long as you can, then put it away for a month.

△ An elaborate talisman made to call on the help of an angel during scrying. It was made by Dr Dee, magician and astrologer to Queen Elizabeth I.

A TALISMAN INVOCATION

The words you use when consecrating the talisman should reflect your purpose, and be directed at the powers you have chosen to make your request to. It is a good idea to forumulate the invocation before you begin the ceremony, but you can also rely on inspiration for the words to come to you at the right time, or use something like the following invocation:

"Lady/Lord of Air (Fire, Water and Earth, in turn), bless this thy symbol, and let power be in dwelling."

Go round all the Elemental symbols and, if possible carry them to each point of the compass, or elevate them in the right direction.

"Great Lady/Lord (name of planet or other force you wish to infuse into the talisman), enter into this oil, that it may bless and dedicate this symbol and give it the power to work effectively in this plane of Earth."

"Spirit that moveth on the face of the waters, wash from this symbol all past associations that it may be pure and dedicated to its new purpose."

You should say the words and sprinkle a few drops of water on the talisman, then sprinkle a little salt upon it and say:

"Lady of Earth, foundation of our lives and work, take away the links of the past, and instil into this talisman the strength and stability that it may perform its true destiny."

A SPELL TO HELP YOU SENSE MAGICALLY

This spell will increase your sensitivity to the magical world and help you to work intuitively.

1 Take a clear glass bowl of warm water and add fresh rosemary sprigs or essential oil of rosemary, rose or lavender. Light a pale blue candle and some jasmine or sandalwood incense.

2 Wash your hands and face in the water, saying "Purify me, Lady of Awakening, that my senses may be clear and true in this hour." Allow your hands to dry in the air.

3 With your fingers straight and pointing up, press your palms together and then gradually draw them apart. Really feel, sense or see the energy between them. When you want to detect a magical object, repeat this with your hands around it for the same result. Say "Thank you" and allow the feeling to fade to normal.

Leaving the Talisman to Work

Sometimes talismans can be carried either in a small pouch made of coloured felt, or they may be placed out of sight, for example on top of a high cupboard, or under a bed. Alternatively, place the talisman under a stone to absorb the stabilizing energy of the Earth. It is important to allow the talisman to work undisturbed, for like a newly planted seed, its power cannot grow if it is always being dug up. Say to yourself, "The power of light will grow in darkness, and my will shall be done" and leave it alone.

After one cycle of the Moon, consider the matter again. If it has worked you will know, but if it hasn't, you have to think if you asked for something you may not have, or if the request was posed in the wrong way.

Talismans for money don't work, because money is not a thing itself, but a medium of exchange. You might ask for a holiday, or a new item of clothing, and you may find after your talisman is made that you are offered work or an exchange of things.

△ Place the completed talisman under a stone so that it can absorb the energy of the Earth.

The Powers of the Planets and

The Days of the Week

Human beings have been fascinated with the lights in the sky since earliest times, if the many ancient artefacts that they have left are anything to go by. Many of the oldest surviving constructions align to the sunrise or sunset, usually at the solstices in December and June. In some settings, these may just be rows of standing stones, or circles of rocks with gaps at these points in the ring. Sometimes a single stone is like the backsight on a rifle, with the foresight being a gap in the surrounding hills or a mountain peak, marking an important rising or setting place for the Sun or Moon.

△ **The stars are seen as symbols of hope, guidance and ancient wisdom in many cultures.**

The Stars

Because these great lights appear to move on cyclic paths, time can be marked by them returning to an earlier place. It is thought that the first henge monuments, which were technically ring ditches and embankments, were fixed observatories. The astronomer would stand in the ditch and have a flat circular horizon against which could be observed the stars or Moon.

Posts could be driven into the top of the bank and so patterns of movement gradually traced over a year or more. The planets are

INCORPORATING SUN AND MOON CYCLES

You may need to look at the phases of the Moon too, because if she is waxing bigger it will help all magic that is concerned with growth and expansion, if she is waning her light will remove blockages, cool fevers or break down barriers. Magic needs to be focused on all the natural tides of the Sun and the Moon, and the more you are able to understand about these ever- flowing energies of construction and dissolution, the more effective your magic will become.

the most useful set of powers to work with as they have well-known and easily described deities associated with them from most parts of the world and, though you will come across a number of different attributes for each one, any set will be acceptable – but should always be used consistently.

The Planets and the Days of the Week

A set of magical correspondences most useful to all witches and magicians are the days of the week. The planets can be learnt from the names of the days. You will need to do further research on the underlying symbolism and arrive at a set of correspondences which, even if they don't agree with anyone else's list, satisfies you. Don't rush this research – it is a long process. From the moment you decide to make a working, you are already involved in the process, and it will not be completed until the aim for which you are working has been accomplished.

SUNDAY

Planet: Sun

Colours: gold/yellow

Number: 6

Incenses: cedar or frankincense

Metal: gold

MONDAY

Planet: Moon

Colours: white/silver

Number: 9

Incenses: jasmine or water lily

Metal: silver

TUESDAY

Planet: Mars (Tiw, Saxon)

Colour: red

Number: 5

Incense: tobacco

Metal: iron

WEDNESDAY

Planet: Mercury (Wotan, Saxon)

Colour: orange

Number: 8

Incense: mastic

Metal: mercury

THURSDAY

Planet: Jupiter (Thor, Saxon)

Colour: royal blue

Number: 4

Incense: cedar wood

Metals: tin or brass

FRIDAY

Planet: Venus (Freya, Saxon)

Colour: green

Number: 7

Incenses: roses or patchouli

Metal: copper

SATURDAY

Planet: Saturn

Colour: black

Number: 3

Incense: myrrh

Metals: lead or pewter

THE DAYS OF THE WEEK

Each day of the week is dedicated to a particular kind of magic.

Sunday

is the day for solar magic which helps your individual self. It is a time when you can work for personal healing or for a new impulse to assist your life.

Monday

is for Moon workings. Her silvery light can be used to strengthen psychic or dreaming powers, to enhance the ability to meditate and to be inspired from your inner depths. There are many Moon goddesses, and even the Egyptian god Thoth is a ruler of moon power, if you want help.

Tuesday

offers Mars energy to end conflicts, to overcome inertia or to deal with those matters that may metaphorically need to be kick started, or have physical work applied to them. It can be a day of passionate feelings or determined efforts that bring results.

Wednesday

is the time for Mercury's powers of communication, to link up with long-lost friends, or write important letters. Mercury or Hermes is the god of thieves, so if something has been stolen from you, now could be the time to seek it out or ask to get it back.

Thursday

is the king of the gods, Jupiter's, day. He rules over business and material growth, justice and legal matters, so if you are taking action to expand your work, or seeking judgement on your affairs, now could be the time.

△ **Light a blue candle for Jupiter.**

Friday

is Venus's day. She is the goddess often associated with love, but she rules over all kinds of partnerships, and harmony and beauty generally. If you want to change your image or purchase a work of art for your home, then Venus can help. She is not a goddess to ask for help if you are wishing someone else to fall in love with you. You can use her powers only for yourself – to try to influence someone else may be leaning towards misuse of magic. If you want love, make yourself lovable.

Saturday

ends the week and is ruled by dark-browed Saturn, father of the gods and ruler of time. His help can be sought for anything to do with old age, with setting up or breaking down boundaries or limitations. His magic works slowly but it can be gentle and extremely powerful, if you have the patience to allow him to work with you.

△ **A gold candle, amber beads, frankincense and solar symbols evoke the healing power of the Sun.**

The Planets and the Hours of the Day

In each day there are also several hours dedicated to each planet's power. They are not clock hours but one-twelfth of the time between local sunrise and sunset, and sunset and sunrise. This means that in summer the day hours are more than 60 minutes long and the night hours less. The first hour of each day from sunrise is dedicated to the planet whose day it is, and the following hours are ruled by the planets in this sequence: Moon, Saturn, Jupiter, Mars, Sun, Venus, Mercury then Moon, Saturn, Jupiter, etc.

From this you can calculate Moon or Mercury hours in any day, should you wish to work on a talisman then. The Moon hour on the Moon day is the strongest available lunar force, especially if it were during the sign of Cancer, for example.

△ **The green colour of the candles attract the power of the planet Venus during a ritual for harmony and love.**

Ideally, to bring in the greatest energies to a talisman, for example, you would also look at the actual planetary positions within the signs of the zodiac, and take into account your own birth sign, and the various aspects between your chosen planets. However, that is a complete area for study on its own. As you follow your magic path you will choose what aspects of knowledge are right for you to study.

Meditation is the passport to
Astral Travel

Ancient mythology contains many valuable stories in which the characters are stars or become stars, in the same way that the Ancient Egyptian Pharaohs were supposed to rise in the heavens and shine with Osiris in the constellation of Orion. These ancient legends are often used in ritual, especially by ceremonial magicians who take on the powers of the gods and goddesses. This is done to allow the spirits of the gods and goddesses as teachers, healers, protectors or guides, to enter today's world and share their power with us. To enable their wisdom to reach us, the most favourable atmosphere has to be set – an inner temple, similar to their own ancient one, must be created and entered fully. The ceremonial magician must then call upon the gods and goddesses and allow them to overshadow him or herself completely.

Meditate to travel

Imagination and magic have the same root, and all draw on what magicians and witches call the "Astral" or starry realms. You could say this is the world we all enter in dream. Sometimes it is very real, very familiar and everyday events occur there. At other times our dreams are wild, bizarre and even otherworldly. Those who walk the paths of witchcraft and magic teach themselves consciously to enter the astral planes and bring back information or power.

Meditation is a key doorway to the inner landscapes, and guided meditation, creative visualization or pathworking all teach the astral traveller how to shift from the outer, mundane level of awareness to the inner, and return safely with a full awareness of what has been observed.

Although the process of sitting still, in silence and relaxation, may seem quite simple, many people with busy lives today may find it extremely difficult. It is a skill that cannot be forced but which must be allowed to work gently. Be patient. Meditation can use symbols drawn from anywhere as a focus, as pictures, words or diagrams.

△ The Egyptians believed that when the Pharaohs died, they travelled to the heavens and became stars. Here Osiris begins his journey.

Theatre and Magic

Not everyone is ready to be directly inspired by the energies of a deity, so sometimes the myths are enacted like a play, so that the recorded words, actions and examples set long ago may be studied again and their content decoded for the modern age. Today we view the theatre mainly as drama for entertainment. However, it started in the temples of ancient Greece where it was the stage for religious instruction. There the stories of the gods, their battles and actions were played out by priests before huge audiences in the great temple amphitheatres, with amazing sounds, lights and stage effects. Into the Christian era, priests started by acting out Christ's passion and the scene with the empty tomb and the angels. Later this was expanded into what became the Mystery Plays, when whole Bible stories were played out by different Craft Guilds, and later still, it became what it is today.

△ Meditation is the doorway to astral travel. Burning incense will help you to achieve the mental state necessary for your journey.

△ Make sure you are sitting comfortably in a straight-backed chair with arms, since your journey may take some time.

△ Mentally travelling through a real or remembered forest is an effective way of reaching other worlds.

MAKING AN ASTRAL JOURNEY

Like many of the other aspects of magic, you will need a quiet time and place. If you are intent on going into the astral levels you will need a reliable companion for basic guidance to share your visions with and help clarify their meaning.

1 Clear a physical and mental space, set up a basic circle and sphere of light around yourself and make the statement "I wish to travel to the astral realms in order to discover…" You should choose a simple target.

2 Sit with your companion nearby. Your friend could speak a narrative leading you to the kind of place in which you imagine what you seek would exist. You have to find the landscape,

which really already exists on the astral plane. Look on it as another continent or a different dimension of space. Acknowledge that it is real, and that, unlike some images you make for yourself, you can't change what you see.

3 Once you have seen the surroundings, which may be sufficient for one day, come back to normal awareness, report to your friend, and close your circle.

4 A second attempt will require a different exercise. Here you need to create your protective circle, but instead of setting off into the other dimension, begin to construct an image of your own body, perhaps dressed in the costume of the astral realm, standing before you, but facing away. In other words, see your own back in front of you. Work on this until you are able really to see it.

5 Once you have built your own figure, you need to transfer your awareness to it, by a kind of mental leap. This immediately puts many people back to themselves, but with gentle effort you

◁ **Many inner journeys can be read by a magical companion to lead the traveller onwards.**

can succeed. You then need to transfer to your "astral self" and insert that self into the inner surroundings so that you can meet your hero or Goddess. For this you may need help from your companion, who will describe the setting when you have indicated that you are in your astral body. What you will experience there is completely real but it has a different look or feel to "real life". With practice over a number of short sessions, most people find that they can do this if they don't force it.

A few short sessions of half an hour are far better than a prolonged attempt of hours.

△ **After any kind of astral experience, a hot drink will help to ground you while you discuss your visions with your guide.**

Meeting Gods and Goddesses on

Inner Journeys

A vivid imagination, directed by magical training, is the most effective tool we have for changing the world, and it is something which has often lain dormant since childhood. The world of myth is still there, but our adult eyes tend to look through it. We can regain the dimmed sight if we so wish, and with it see infinity, explore the far side of the Moon, visit the lands of lost legend and draw on the power that lies there.

Making an Inner Journey

Here is an imaginary journey to a place that is peaceful, powerful and magical, and where it is easy to sink into an altered state of aware-ness to commune with the inner beings. Get into a meditative frame of mind, and make sure you will not be disturbed for about half an hour. If possible, record the narrative on tape, pausing after every sentence to allow the images to build up, or get a friend to read it to you, or go through it a number of times until you can recall the various stages. Allow the images to become as real as possible.

The journey is to the Hall of the Gods, where you will be able to insert your images of the God or Goddess. Try these one at a time, until you are really able to see, feel, sense and appreciate their presence.

You are creating the pictures partly from memory or imagination, and partly because they are real in another realm or dimension. Of course you can share the experience with your friends.

1 You may like to light a candle and open a circle of protection, perform the self-blessing or otherwise make yourself ready.

2 Sit upright, close your eyes and concen-trate on your breathing. Allow it to slow down and become deeper.

3 Begin to build up a picture of an elaborate doorway; see the frame and the details of the closed door. What is it made of? What does it feel like to the touch? How can it be opened? This is the door from your world to the realm of the Gods.

There may be a guardian who is there to enquire who you are and why you wish to go through, or to ask for a password, a token or sign. You will have to find your own answers.

4 After a few moments, as you continue to relax and make the experience deeper, you will find that the door can be opened. At first a great light seems to be shining through the doorway, and you stand on the threshold while your inner vision adjusts.

5 The light dims so that you can look into the place beyond, and what you see is a glorious hall, built of golden stone. Upon the walls are paintings or hangings picked out in bright colours. You step forward on to a paved floor covered in mosaics. Everything you see is on a grand scale. The ceiling is high above but that too is painted and gilded, and everything is beautiful. To one side of the room there is a platform reached by several steps covered with marvellous brocade, and on the dais is a throne, carved and covered in gold.

△ Use illustrations and works of art to inspire and direct your personal vision.

Upon it you start to make out a figure that is both awe-inspiring but also somehow approachable.

6 You move towards the steps and try to make out the face of the figure seated above you. (At this point you will need to insert the description of the deity you wish to meet, as described to the right.)

7 When you have had your audience with the deity, taking as long as you need, always give thanks, even if the advice is not immediate, and act with respect.

8 Allow the image of the great hall to fade, so that you see again the door and threshold. The light dims and gently you return to your own place.

9 Unwind your circle slowly, allowing your memory to recall every detail.

△ **A simple enlightening ritual can help you discover the art of exploring inner realms.**

PICTURING THE DEITY

These descriptions should help you picture your chosen deity as you travel on your inner journey.

Apollo

The Sun God, Apollo is seen as a very beautiful mature man. His skin shines like sunlight and upon his head is a radiant crown which blazes with brilliant light. He is wrapped in a swathe of golden cloth, the end of which falls to his feet, on which he wears golden sandals. In his hands he holds a small harp or lyre. He looks at you and smiles. A feeling of warmth and welcome surrounds you, and you feel able to ask for his help or guidance.

Diana

The Moon Goddess, Diana or Artemis, stands at the top of the steps. She is a lithe-limbed young woman, lightly dressed in a short tunic of fine leather. At her side is a large hunting dog. She seems to shine with a silvery light and a strange coolness is in the air. Diana reaches her hand out to you, and you take it, finding her fingers cool and firm. You experience a shift of awareness as if some deep part of your mind is waking up. You ask for her help or inspiration.

Mercury

Mercury or Hermes has a boyish figure; it is hard to tell if he is truly male or female. He is laughing and light-hearted, yet his face shows cunning; you can tell he is a trickster. He wears a short tunic of silvery material, and on his feet are winged sandals, and in his hand he carries a wand. It is a staff entwined by two snakes, one black and the other white and they seem to move. Mercury asks why you have come, how he can communicate with you or lead you on your travels.

Venus

Venus or Aphrodite, or the Egyptian Goddess Hathor, may be seen as a beautiful woman in a long dress. She carries a flower, perhaps a rose or a lotus, and its scent lifts your spirits. Your heart leaps with love, and powerful emotions sweep through you. You want to fall at her feet and weep or laugh with joy. You control your feelings and mentally frame a request for more love, harmony and peace in your life. Gently she smiles down at you, raises you up and offers you her flower.

Jupiter

Jupiter, Jove or Zeus is the Father of the Gods, an older man seated on the throne and robed in dark blue. His hair is curly and has touches of grey but he is ruggedly handsome and you sense his power. In his hand is a rod of power or command and you go forward carefully and with respect as if you were meeting a great statesman. You know he will help but you have to be very precise in what you ask.

Saturn

Saturn or Cronus is the great Lord of Time and Creation, and he wears a black robe. His face is stern and wrinkled, and his hair is white and crowned with a laurel wreath. He sits still and silently brooding. Leaning against the throne is a scythe and an hourglass. You slowly approach the steps and politely ask for his help. He smiles and it is clear he will assist you.

△ ▷ **Ancient sacred places can be used as gateways to the other worlds. By mentally building such images, you can move through time and space.**

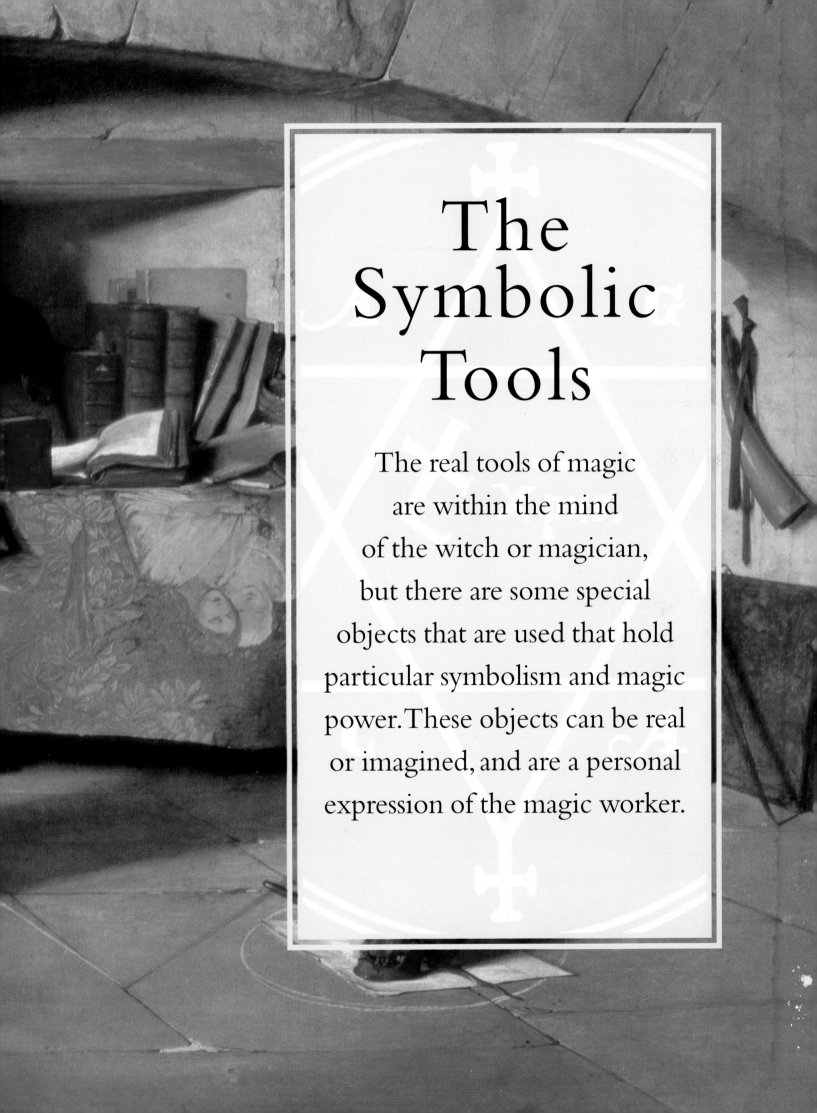

The Symbolic Tools

The real tools of magic
are within the mind
of the witch or magician,
but there are some special
objects that are used that hold
particular symbolism and magic
power. These objects can be real
or imagined, and are a personal
expression of the magic worker.

Making and creating
Sacred Spaces and Circles

Before performing any magic, a witch or magician needs to create the right atmosphere and environment in which to work. In order to do this, they need to prepare themselves and the place in which they are going to work. To prepare for any kind of celebration, ritual or magical work the witch or magician will perform a simple act of connection to the Gods and Goddesses they work with.

△ **The Earth, our home and Mother.**

In the same way that someone might make the sign of the cross when entering church, the magic worker will say a brief invocation, calling upon the highest powers to purify the intent, focus the worker on the work in hand and acknowledge the forces of Nature. This ritual might involve a symbolic gesture, such as drawing a circle in the air, while saying a brief invocation. The words of an invocation are personal and can take any form, but might be similar to the following words: "I am a Child of Earth but my heritage is among the stars of Heaven. Around me stand the four gateways of the Elements, of Earth and Water, Fire and Air, and in the centre burns my heart with love. May the great Goddess bless my working, and may the great God protect and support me. So may this be." Most people develop their own words, or have several variations, perhaps mentioning other aspects of the four elements with which they work, or naming a particular Goddess and God under whose auspices they are performing their ceremony.

Creating a Sacred Space

Ideally, inner work is performed in a special place, which may be somewhere set aside for the work in or out of doors, or it may be created for the moment of use anywhere. You may wish to set up a suitable temple, laboratory, workshop or grove, depending on which sphere you most wish to delve into. You may be interested in ritual or the arts of making talismans. You might wish to study healing or draw nearer the God and Goddesses of the pagan faith; you may prefer simple meditation and the gentle ways of pathworking or the study of lost knowledge and its application in today's more technological times. Your individual purposes will to a certain extent influence the way your magical place is designed in the real world, although you can change its inner appearance and structure at will.

△ **The interface between the land and the ocean, and day and night, is especially sacred.**

Choosing Your Sacred Space

Initially you may simply prefer to study books about other sacred spaces, such as ancient temples, stone circles, pyramids and similar structures. Perhaps you can visit some of these places, absorb their special atmosphere and bring back pictures to help you remember them.

Perhaps you prefer to design the ideal layout on paper, or make a model temple that you can enter, in your imagination, rearranging the furniture or symbols according to the purpose or season. Perhaps you can make an outdoor shrine in your garden, or in the countryside where you and your companions may gather for festivals, or maybe you are limited to using some small corner of your bedroom to set out a display of relevant items, or where you can light a candle to sit and meditate.

Whatever symbolism and material you have chosen, you will soon find that every ounce of effort was worthwhile, and that the time involved will quickly be repaid once you begin to make use of this "other place" that you have created. Gradually you will find its atmosphere changes, and that simply to enter the place, adopt the robes, regalia, or even the frame of mind in which magic is a reality, will cause you to shift into that altered gear where your power and understanding may be awesome.

If you are able to have a permanent sacred space, you will have to make some choices. Because this work is concerned with developments in practical magic, your final place may be the result of experiments which you have not yet tried, and so the pattern may need to remain flexible and open at present. This might even be how it stays.

In any case, you will need enough space and flexibility for you and your companions to be able to sit together comfortably and, if possible, move around a central table, altar or workbench.

Creating a Magical Circle

Wherever you work, it is traditional to create a magical circle. Whether you are working inside or out you should visualize this as a place of stillness beyond normal time and space. The circle may be outlined with a wand or staff, but as you turn round, drawing a line in the air, you may see it burning with golden fire. It will help you concentrate on your work, and will banish any unwanted thoughts or influences. With practice, you will come to know it is there, protective and empowering, each time you begin your ritual.

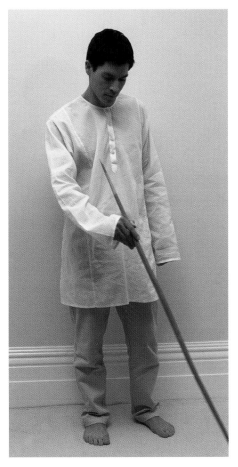

△ Some magicians and witches use a wand to create a "place between the worlds".

△ A witch may direct blessing power through his or her hand to make a magic circle.

△ The working place is a circle of light, whether visualized or made with physical artefacts.

Making Your Circle Magical

Magical circles normally also recognize the four directions of the compass: North is the place of Earth; West is the place of the watery region; South has the heat of Fire and East possesses the breath of Air. These may be marked around your magic circle with an appropriate coloured candle which you should light as you begin your spell.

Some people call upon guardians of the quarters, who may be seen as Archangels, totem animals, Gods and Goddesses, Holy Living Creatures, or any other kind of otherworld beings. These powerful guardians will be with you during your work and should be thanked respectfully, rather than dismissed, at the end.

△ Often a circle has to be created within the square structure of a room, a temple or a field, for example.

SEATING

Choose your seating with care, as many meditations, pathworking trips and certain experiments in time and astral travel will require you to remain relaxed and passive for some considerable lengths of time. Therefore, comfort and convenience are important. Looking at what is readily available, some of the high-backed "garden" chairs make ideal magical thrones. If you want the throne to fit a particular colour scheme, you can use a cloth or blanket to cover it. These chairs are light to move about, and will fold up when not in use.

Cauldrons, broomsticks, wands and pentacles –
A Witch's Tools

An old term for a magician, or magic worker, is "wizard". Traditionally, these were thought of as men, but in fact they could be either male or female, as is the case with witches today. Remember that the tools here differ from those of a ceremonial magician, whose four magical instruments are the pentacle, chalice, sword and wand. There are a number of objects associated with workers of magic which, though they may now seem archaic, have a number of functions that have not been bettered. After you have created your sacred space, you need to equip it with these appropriate tools.

△ **A candle in a cauldron represents Fire.**

The Cauldron

One such object is the traditional witch's iron cauldron. Cauldrons are meeting places of all four Elements, used in nearly all traditions of practical magic. The iron pot is for Earth, the fluid within for Water, the burning wood or peat below for Fire, and the rising steam and scents for Air. In medieval times most cooking was done over an open fire in an iron cauldron. The cauldron was at

MAKING A WAND

Witches use simple wands – a hazel stick carved with a spiral and bound with a ribbon. Ceremonial magicians use a more elaborate wand, designed around the symbolism of the signs of the zodiac.

To make one of these yourself you will need:

A dowel, about 1.5 cm (⅝ in) thick and about 1 m (1 yd) long
A selection of brilliant paints in the colours of the rainbow plus black, white and gold. These may be poster paints, enamels or any other bright modern paints.
Some thin card or even metal or plastic
Varnish if you want to make the finished wand more durable.

1 Paint a wide white band at the top of the stick of the wand and paint the other end of the shaft black.

2 Between the black and white, paint 12 bands starting with scarlet, orange, yellow, green, blue.

3 While the paint is drying make the water lily for the top. This is made with three layers of the card, metal or plastic, cut into petals, painted with gold, and a green layer of sepals beneath.

the centre of the home, hanging over the fire in the hearth, which had to be regularly tended and stoked up with fuel. It was often the focus of the women in the household's life, providing nourishment and inner wisdom. Some women were sensitive to the strange patterns which might be seen in the swirling water, and some could see the future, or events happening far away. Today many witches who do not have a hearth in their homes will light a candle in a cauldron to represent the hearth fire of old. Often, instead of a cauldron they will have a chalice or goblet, at least as a symbol of the cauldron.

△ **A chalice or cup is sometimes used as a symbol of the cauldron.**

The Broomstick

The besom or traditional broomstick was another vital piece of household equipment. It was made up of materials which were easy to come by, and many lands have their own simple versions. In Europe many besoms were made with birch twigs for the bristles, a handle of hazel, and originally a binding of willow withies. Each of these plants has magical associations, birch often being seen as a tree linked to birth and beginnings, hazel to wisdom or far seeing, and willow to the healing of the old Crone Goddess. The whole implement is used domestically for sweeping the floor, and magically for clearing out any disturbances from a place used as a magical circle. In the days of earth floors, a circle would literally be swept clear and obvious in the dust, and this ring would form the limits of magical work. It would form a visible barrier to the inner realm and a protection against any outside influences that might disrupt the work within.

Sometimes today witches still sweep the area they use for magic, and may place the

△ The cauldron has been linked with witches for centuries, but was in fact simply a universal cooking pot.

besom on the edge of the ritual circle to form a doorway through which their companions may enter the sacred ring.

The Wand

Wands are traditionally associated with wizards and are still much used by modern magic workers. The simplest kind is a straight stick from which the bark may have been cut in a spiral or other pattern. It may be carved or painted, but basically it is a pointer, to direct the will of the wizard outwards. Sometimes a wand is used to mark a magical circle, by scratching a mark, or it may be held outwards, marking a circle in the air, to create the "Place that is between the worlds of time and space" where all real magic is performed.

The Pentacle

The pentacle, a five-pointed star, is a symbol that has been closely associated with different kinds of magic and with religious symbolism for thousands of years. It has been found painted on the walls of ancient temples, carved on the stones of churches by the masons constructing them and used as the pattern of many stained-glass windows in old cathedrals. The five points are sometimes seen as symbolizing the head, hands and feet of the witch, and it is thought that the proportions link up with the Golden Mean, a very ancient sacred measurement. Sometimes witches wear this symbol as a pendant or on a ring, usually made of or painted in silver, as this is traditionally the metal of the Moon, the pagans' goddess.

△ Witches were thought to be able to make astral journeys on broomsticks.

△ Make a wand by binding ribbon around it and then carving the spiral shape with a knife.

△ A pentacle can be made from twigs, bound in the correct shape and then sprayed silver.

Making and choosing your own
Shrine and Incense

You have now created your sacred space and equipped it with the tools you will need. The next step is to provide a shrine for it, for which you will need to choose symbols and, to evoke the right atmosphere, burn incense.

Creating a Shrine

An altar is set out specifically for each piece of work, but a more permanent display is a shrine. This will help you focus on your meditations, or show to your family and friends the symbols of the festival or season. In this case a small corner or table top can be set out as a shrine. Here you place a statue of the Gods and Goddesses you honour, or a picture of an Angel or other sacred symbol.

Whatever is put here must be meaningful to you, not just picked out of a book. You can arrange flowers and representations of the magical Moon, or the nearest sacred festival, and change these as time passes. If you prefer, you can set up something in the garden, which is usually called a grotto, rather than a shrine. This is bigger and should have growing flowers and herbs, larger rocks, pieces of sea-washed wood or other pleasing items.

SYMBOLS FOR YOUR ALTAR

When you are working magic, either as a witch or a magician, you will need to set out an altar with symbols which represent the four Elements of Earth, Water, Fire and Air.

Earth

Air

The simplest layout is a stone for Earth, a glass bowl of Water, a lighted red candle for Fire and either some scented flowers, a feather, joss sticks or real incense for Air. Most people have a selection of favourite objects which can be dedicated to use in magical work.

Water

Fire

Small shrines, displaying seasonal symbols, are constructed to celebrate each full moon or festival. For complete rituals there are other Elemental objects added to your altar. These include a centre lamp, a cup of wine or fruit juice and a platter of bread and sometimes salt, which are drunk and eaten as part of the sacred meal during ritual, and some incense grains burned on charcoal.

Incense

There are many crafts involved in practical magic, and one of these is choosing incenses for your work. Sometimes a special blend of scents is made for a particular ritual or festival, and on other occasions any pleasant smell is used. A small amount may be burned when you meditate. It is worth learning a little about incense as it is one of the oldest and most pleasant offerings you can use. In ancient temples, it was burned to carry the prayers and requests of the worshippers to the gods and goddesses above. Most incenses are a mixture of gums, resins, flower petals, wood shavings and oils. Each flavour is dedicated to a particular magical or planetary force, and a little of this symbolism should be learned if you want to blend your own incenses.

△ The simplest of shrines can be made from a Goddess figure, a candle and a single flower.

△ Incense comes in the form of resins, gums and crystals, as well as the familiar sticks and cones.

△ **Dried herbs, such as sage, rosemary and bay, as well as cinnamon quills and juniper berries, can be used in your personal incense mixtures.**

Making Solar Incense

To make a special incense for any occasion you will need a pestle and mortar, as the gums often come in quite big lumps and it is the best way to blend all the ingredients. For a solar incense, used during any healing ritual, or to celebrate a Solstice or Equinox:

1 Take about a teaspoon of frankincense, with some crushed cinnamon quill, some marigold petals and a few drops of honey and orange oil.

2 Mix well in the mortar, so that the texture is like breadcrumbs used in baking.

3 Ideally, this mixture should be allowed to blend for a few hours, then a little can be burned on hot charcoal.

BURNING INCENSE

If you are not used to using incense and are not familiar with how to burn it, follow these guidelines.

1 Use the special charcoal blocks that are sold by occult supply houses. Use a heatproof stand or container and a perforated metal mesh stand; you can make one from a jam jar lid with holes punched in it. This allows air to circulate under the charcoal keeping it alight.

2 Light the charcoal with a match and leave for a few moments. Once the charcoal is hot, sprinkle on a very small amount of the incense mixture. To begin with a mere pinch will be enough to discover whether you like the smell and how much smoke it is giving off.

▷ **Incense must be burned in fireproof containers and not left unattended.**

Choosing Your Incense

You will find that a number of books give recipes for different incenses. Some contain spices such as star anise, cinnamon, cloves and dried ginger; others have herbs, rosemary, sage, basil stems, southernwood, and other aromatic plants. Some incenses contain non-scented items like crushed seashells for a marine incense, or pretty seeds or colouring materials. Some of these don't smell particularly nice when heated, so take care.

There are plenty of suppliers of different specialized incense mixtures worldwide, as many religions still use these in their liturgies. These church incenses may be too heavy for witchcraft rituals, but a small amount of some can form the basis for a special blend, because they do burn well and safely. If you have the chance to try out single-scented incenses one at a time you will soon learn what you like, which evoke the kinds of powers you require, and which you don't like. Gather materials and keep them dry in sealed containers, clearly marked with the contents.

It really is an ancient craft to blend your own incenses, and with a little experience you can create a selection of scents that will conjure up just the right mood and atmosphere for any ritual or celebration.

3 Materials that you have dried yourself, such as resin from pine trees, shavings of wood from pitch pine, apple, cedar or sandalwood, can also be added. The stems of many culinary herbs including rosemary, sage or fennel, burn quite well if they are dry.

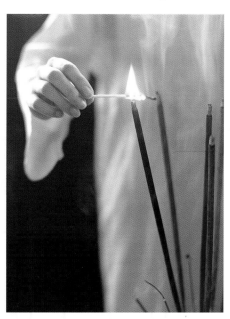

△ **The scent used for every ritual should align to its purpose.**

A WORD OF WARNING

Always be very careful when burning incenses not only because of the heat of burning charcoal and the container, but also because some people react badly to the smoke from incenses. Anyone who has asthma or breathing difficulties should be very cautious when burning materials. Myrrh and dittany of Crete, for example, both give off a lot of smoke.

Magical equipment –
Robes and Temple Furniture

Equipping your sacred space involves not only tools such as cups and swords, but also furniture such as a table and chairs. And you will also need a robe for yourself.

△ Those who have worked magic from earliest times have worn special robes and used ancient symbols that are still part of a magician's inherited wisdom today.

△ You will need a straight-backed chair with arms, and a table for your equipment.

△ Make a collection of coloured silks and fabrics for your magic work.

Temple Furniture and Equipment

In the last generation of magical temples, the Elemental weapons played an important role in consecration, rituals and symbolism. Most magicians collected a cup and a sword, created or painted a pentacle and dedicated a wand, in accordance with the Key of Solomon or the instructions derived from the Order to which they belonged. Each of these instruments has many layers of symbolism and you may wish to follow this well-trodden path of earlier magical practice.

An alternative which might align closer to the purposes of Aquarian magic is to find a cup which you will need for the wine or water, and to make a personal pentagram, showing your magical aims and mirroring your current state of advancement. Swords have always been difficult to find or expensive to buy, complicated to make and embarrassing to carry about if you are not performing your rituals at home. Although it is possible to get a fake sword to hang on the wall or wave about during ceremonies, it might not feel right for everyone. Decide what you want for the sorts of rituals you intend to perform.

Other temple or sanctuary furniture should always be chosen for its practicality, rather than paying a lot of money for fancy items that don't work well when used.

As few people these days have space to set aside a full-time sacred area in their homes, equipment may have to serve dual or multiple roles in the household. You will need a table for an altar, a comfortable and supportive chair for meditations and inner work, and some kind of cupboard, chest or box in which to keep equipment when not in use. If you decide to set out a shrine to celebrate the changing seasons or Moons, you will need a small area to place a few flowers, symbols, statues or pictures which can reflect the patterns of your own land and surroundings.

Magical Robes

A special robe or other ceremonial costume is quite important to the working of magic. Although many people do just wear clean clothes for rituals, actually changing into a dedicated robe after setting aside your usual attire can be psychologically very effective. Traditional robes are simple T-shaped garments, reaching to the ankles, and with long sleeves, in the manner of a kaftan or kimono. Ideally they are made by the wearer from natural fibres, such as cotton, silk, linen or wool. Some groups have a specific colour or design, but for working on your own or with friends, a simple garment in any design will be fine. Some people like to embroider or decorate their robes; some have long sleeves which are wide or fairly tight (safer when dealing with lit candles and fire); others are sleeveless or short sleeved.

MAKING A ROBE

Robes may be made from a pattern found in stage-costume books, or that of historical dress, but really all that is needed is a piece of material that reaches from neck to heels, and is wide enough to make two matching pieces for the front and back. The most basic robe can just be a tube of material, with armholes but no sleeves, and a simple neckline that is big enough to get your head through. Obviously the actual design will depend on how much skill you have at dress-making, and how much time and effort you wish to spend on decoration.

△ Traditionally, robes are ankle length and made of natural materials, as wearing a special garment helps us to set aside our everyday selves.

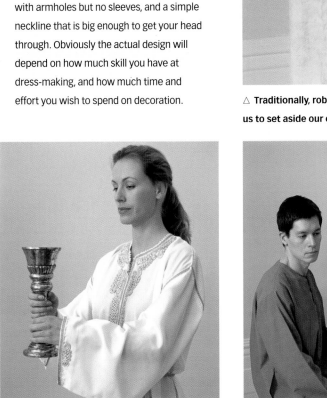

△ A particular colour may be what you want for a certain spell or ritual; gold is much used in magic.

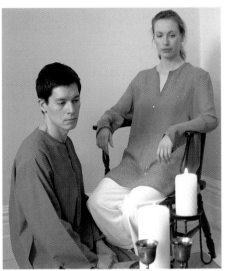

△ Sometimes just clean and comfortable clothes are all that are needed during simple rites.

△ Regalia may be elaborate or as simple as this stole, worn for meditation or study.

The next step –
Candle Spells and Journeys

Your sacred space is ready and fully equipped with the tools and furnishings you have created and chosen. You now have somewhere you can start practising magic.

△ **The magician is one who reaches beyond the limits of our everyday world, yet keeps in contact with the ground. Meditation and visualization are ways in which we can travel to other worlds.**

with their own efforts and on them. Getting physically well again may only be one small step on a long path to total recovery, and help and support will be required of the magic worker all through that process.

Once you have made up your mind exactly what you intend to achieve by using candle magic you will need to set out a place to work, find a suitable new candle and holder, and perhaps prepare a symbol of what you aim to achieve. To make the spell especially effective, it is worth sitting down quietly and following the narrative of an inner journey.

This will mentally guide you, and any companions, to the place best suited to the particular sort of magic you need. If you think about it, every kind of inner work has a natural home. The arts of the old village witch suit a country cottage or perhaps its herb garden, which can be clearly imagined as the backdrop to your candle spell. If you were trying to get a different job you might want to mentally conjure up your desired working environment and people it with the kind of colleagues you wish to meet.

Candle Spells

One form of basic magic that is quite easy to do is casting spells using candles. A spell is a set of words which may be sung, chanted or spoken, that asks for a specific kind of change to come about. Getting the words right is an important part of the art of working magic. If you are asking for something to happen to another person you will need their specific permission to work on their behalf. Many people think that healing is always good and no one needs to give permission for healing spells to be performed, but any magic will cause a change for which the magician is responsible. Healing can take many forms, some of which are unpleasant and may require a lot of effort on the part of the patient. Being involved even at a distance from the healing spell opens the sufferer to the power of healing, so that it can work

ANOINTING A CANDLE

A candle is often used as the focus for magic, and it needs to be prepared.

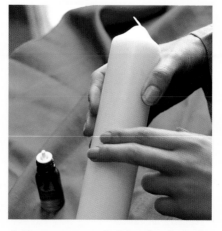

1 Choose a new candle. Take a few drops of essential oil and anoint the candle with it, by stroking upwards with two fingers. Use an oil that corresponds with the spell.

2 As you concentrate on your aim, wind a length of narrow ribbon around the candle to bind your intention to it. Then use the candle in a ritual to accomplish your will.

Inner Journeys

Here is a basic inner journey which will help you to make your candle spells especially effective. Build pictures of each part of the journey as clearly as you can, by either imagining the scene as described, or remembering a similar scene from your own past.

1 Begin by sitting upright in a comfortable chair, with the candle and holder and some matches set out before you. When you have immersed yourself in the inner journey, light your candle and speak your spell.

2 Take a few slow deep breaths to calm and focus yourself, close your eyes and picture the journey as clearly as you can in images, feelings, smells, and other perceptions.

3 You are walking in a beautiful park or garden on a sunny afternoon. It is full of brilliant flowers of many kinds, and you hear the soft hum of bees and feel the wind blowing gently through the leaves. It is very peaceful, yet you are excited. You know you are in a magical place.

4 You are following a path which winds between the flowers. It is smooth and easy to stroll along. In the distance you start to make out a small white temple, raised up on three steps of pale stone. You follow the path until you arrive at the temple.

5 Looking up, you see that you stand before a small classical temple, with a row of six pillars of slender, ribbed stone across the front, forming a portico. You climb the three steps and pass between the central pillars. Beneath your feet there is white stone, and before you is a door of dark wooden panels.

6 You go towards the door and feel the ancient wood and how it must have been polished by the touch of many hands. There are dark iron hinges and an iron latch which you raise. You push on the heavy door and it begins to swing inwards. Beyond it you step into a place of light.

7 When you can see clearly again, you realize that you have entered a circular hall with a domed roof. In the centre of the hall is a circle of tall candles of every colour of the rainbow, set quite wide enough apart to walk between. You enter the ring of lighted candles and are drawn to one particular colour. (If you are working a planetary candle spell, you will be drawn to the appropriate colour.) You stand before it and are almost dazzled by the brightness of the flame and the richness of the colour of the candle itself. It stands as tall as yourself, supported in a shining candlestick, and burns with a bright and steady flame.

8 Within the flame you notice a myriad of different shades of gold and white and scarlet and orange. Gradually you become aware of another presence, and begin to make out a shadowy figure standing beyond the candle. A voice speaks in your head. "I am the spirit of the candle and I burn to assist you."

9 You may see the spirit as a living flame, or as a classical angel, with upraised wings the colour of fire, or as shards of shifting rainbow light in a vague human form. You realize that the form doesn't matter and you ask the spirit for help in your candle spell. You are able to ask specifically for what you need, expressing it clearly. After a while the light seems to fade, the figure grows more indistinct, but you are left with a feeling of profound peace. The knowledge that you will be helped is strong.

10 Again you look around at the circle of candles and now they seem less bright. Beyond them you see the open door and the sunlight shining outside. You turn to leave the circle, silently giving thanks for the offer of help. You feel a sense of blessing wrapping around you as you walk to the door. You pass out to the portico with its tall pillars, and descend the steps slowly.

11 Before you the path stretches away into the beautiful garden which led you to this temple of flame. You walk slowly, again sensing the flowers and their scents and the breeze in the leaves. After a few steps the path and garden begin to be hidden by a mist. This swirls around you, gently guiding you back to your familiar room. Pause for a moment to get your bearings.

12 Now you can light your physical candle and again ask for the help you need. Remain still and open to any guidance which may come to you from the being of flame. Observe the actual candle flame as this may nod or expand, bow or quaver in a simple form of communication. Take your time, again communing with the candle flame.

13 When you are sure you have done everything you can, snuff out the candle so that you can use it again. Return things to their proper places, and stretch and move about to complete the exercise.

14 Write a brief diary note of what help you requested and how clear the vision appeared.

△ **Concentrating on a candle flame in a ritual can help you achieve mental stillness and poise.**

Food and drink
Ritual Bread and Wine

The ritual of preparing and sharing food and drink is an important element in the practice of many kinds of magic. There is a myriad of recipes to choose from for use in your own rituals, but a few examples are given here.

All over the world there are special dishes which are served at festival times throughout the year. These can range from a simple kind of special bread eaten occasionally to elaborate feasts of many courses, chosen to celebrate some national or religious event. In some places there used to be a taboo on eating a certain thing, usually an animal or bird. But once a year, that food was carefully prepared and eaten, as a special mark of respect to the animal, or to the gods of the country. Some of these taboos came about as a result of common sense. Today we have rules about hygiene, refrigeration and safe cooking methods to prevent food poisoning, but in the past people only had salt and sugar as preservatives, or dried or smoked food to make it keep.

△ **In many traditions, food or drink are blessed before being shared in a ceremony.**

Choosing Your Ingredients

As it is traditional all over the world to have special food at festivals, here are some basic recipes that you can adapt to your own needs. Ideally you should always use natural, organic, locally grown and seasonal foods, and those that you have grown yourself are even more special. We are all what we eat, and the plants and animals, the milk and honey are all gifts of the Great Mother Earth, so by sharing her bounty in ritual we are also taking in some of the eternal blessing of creation.

△ **The agape, or sacred meal, traditionally included fruits of the earth.**

△ **With ritual food, it is possible to absorb the essence of four Elements.**

Meals as Rituals

Really all meals should become sacraments, so that whether you eat alone or with friends or family, sharing a meal that you have prepared is sharing a spiritual source of nourishment too.

Perhaps you may feel that you would like to make one meal a month, at the new Moon for example, an opportunity to share some simple dishes with others on your path, to discuss the arts of magic, and celebrate the passing seasons. It can be a time when you decorate your shrine with new flowers and symbols, and use that as the centrepiece of your gathering.

▷ **Offering a cup of water is a very ancient symbol of respect or friendship.**

MAKING FOOD FOR RITUALS

Although for rituals many people just use commercial bread broken into pieces, and any kind of wine, mead, cider or fruit juice as a drink, you may wish to try the old ways where special biscuits or scones and your own wines are made for rituals. You can adapt these recipes, adding your favourite nuts or dried fruits, or anything that seems appropriate.

Although not every one has time to make wines for rituals, it is a pleasing skill to master. Sterilise all the equipment before use. Country wines can be made with fruits, vegetables, herbs, berries and dried fruits.

Country Ginger Wine
You will need:
165 g/5½ oz fresh root ginger
450 g/1 lb sultanas
water to make up 4½ litres/8 pints/20 cups
900 g/2 lb sugar
1.5 ml/¼ tsp of yeast extract
120 ml/4 fl oz/½ cup of strong tea
5 oranges
1 packet all-purpose wine yeast
wine-making bucket, with lid
fermentation vessel with airlock, from wine-making supplier

1 Crush the ginger and rinse the sultanas in warm water, drain and chop and add to ginger in bucket and cover.

2 Heat 550 ml/18 fl oz/2½ cups water in large pot, add sugar and yeast extract and stir until dissolved.

3 Allow this to cool then add it to the bucket with the tea and the juice from the oranges. Add the packet of wine yeast, and top up with cold water to make 4½ litres/8 pints/20 cups.

4 Make sure the bucket is covered between actions, and that there is room for frothing at the top.

5 Store in a warm place for 10 days, stirring twice a day.

6 Rack the liquid from the solids into a fermentation jar and top up with cold water.

7 Insert airlock, and leave to ferment for about 5 weeks at a temperature of about 18°C/65°F.

8 After fermentation has ceased, strain wine into a clean jar.

9 Bottle after about 8 months as the longer the wine is left to mature the clearer and better the flavour.

A basic scone or soft bread
You will need:
225 g/8 oz self-raising flour
5 ml/1 tsp sugar
25 g/1 oz butter
75 ml/5 tbsp milk
30 ml/2 tbsp water
a little salt

Some dried fruits or nuts or spices may be added, or the sugar could be left out and replaced with cheese or spices.

1 Sift the flour and salt into a bowl, add the sugar and rub in the butter until the mixture resembles breadcrumbs. Mix the liquids in and beat to a soft dough.

2 Knead the dough for 3 minutes, then pat out rather than roll until about 2 cm (¾ in) thick.

3 Cut out small circles, about 5 cm (2 in) across, and lift them on to a well-greased baking sheet.

4 Lightly brush the tops with milk and put into a preheated oven at 230°C/450°F/Gas 8.

5 Bake for 10 to 15 minutes until golden brown.

△ The cup and its contents are blessed by those participating in the ritual.

△ Deep draughts of the consecrated wine are taken to absorb its power.

Marking the Cycle of the Year

Witches and magic workers are linked to the lands on which they live, drawing power from the turning year, marking the sacred seasons. The seasons, traditions and festivals vary from place to place – some times are worldwide, such as full and new moons, but solstices and the seasons are not.

Festivals of Candlemas, Easter and the

Spring Equinox

Within the modern pagan community there is a series of seasonal celebrations, some of which are thought to be very ancient, whereas others have left little trace in folklore. However, it is a way of dividing the year into sections to mark the passing of time, and an excuse to celebrate part of the annual story with ritual and group work. Although many of these feasts are particularly important to the wiccans, the old-fashioned village witches would have been involved with their communities in helping with the animals, or bringing in the harvest, and so would have shared in the feasts. They would have advised the farmers and shepherds on forthcoming weather conditions, or the state of the soil for planting, and helped animals give birth.

Festivals of Spring

The oldest feasts are linked with the Goddess and the God as parts of a story in which their lives reflect those of Nature, but because of climate, location and local soil these vary quite a bit from what the books say. Anyway, the festivals that celebrate the changing seasons, or traditional events in the life of the Mother Goddess should happen when Nature herself sets the date. In the past, people did not have written calendars but used the passing seasons to mark time.

Candlemas or the Feast of St Brigit

This is when the Goddess is welcomed back after the birth of her Son/Sun at Yuletide. It is the time for looking for the first spring flowers, usually snowdrops, whose white and green petals show they are linked with the White Goddess, Brede or Brigit, a goddess of smithcraft, poetry and healing. People welcomed her into their houses at the first signs of spring, and candles would be lit in the dark house to encourage light and life.

In a ritual, the youngest daughter of the house would come in, wrapped in a dark cloak, and be welcomed and placed in the seat of honour.

△ **Candlemas celebrates longer days and the return of the light, often shown in rituals by lots of candles.**

She would open her cloak to show a dish of earth with the first flowers and a small candle, from whose flame all the family would take a light to other candles, sharing the light so it burned very bright.

In the Christian church, the 2nd February is called Candlemas, as it is the day the priest blesses the candles for the whole year. It was thought that by this time it would be possible to work a whole day without having to light a candle to see by.

On the farms, the first lambs might be born early in February, and the Celtic name of the festival, Oimelc (imbolc) or Ewe's milk comes from this. A drink called "Lambs' wool" is made by baking an apple in the fire and then dropping it into cider so that it turns fluffy and warms the drink.

△ **Writing resolutions for the new year used to be done at the Spring Equinox. Make a ritual out of this yourself, perhaps making the paper you have written on into a talisman.**

The Feast of St Valentine

On 14th February is the Feast of St Valentine, a time when lovers in many parts of the world exchange gifts or cards, often anonymously. Information about the original saint is scarce but it was thought that before being martyred, he left a message to his beloved signed "your loving Valentine", and this started a trend that continues to this day. Originally this occasion was thought to be when wild birds paired off and started nesting, so it is a time for weddings and betrothals.

△ The burgeoning flowers of spring encourage the heart and bring healing to the weary soul.

△ Rituals in spring use gold and yellow to strengthen the power of the Sun.

The Spring Equinox

Next in the year is the Spring Equinox when the sun moves into the sign of Aries, and day and night are equal. It is a time of balance and looking forward to the growing year. Many seeds, especially wheat, were sown now the soil was warmed after winter. In magical lodges the solar dates are quite important and the equinoxes were often times of initiation, or when the passwords and symbols were changed, and officers moved to a new position. The Christian church has the feast of Easter on the first Sunday after the full Moon after the Spring Equinox, again showing that the church incorporated an ancient pattern of festivals into its own calendar, setting the date by the Moon, rather than the fixed date.

Spring Resolutions

As the days lengthen it is a good time to make a promise to yourself, perhaps writing it down and placing it on your spring shrine, about the work you intend to accomplish in the coming months. As the year turns the sunlight can encourage your efforts and make your magic more powerful. This is especially true if you connect yourself to Nature and work with her tides of growth and harvest.

SYMBOLS OF EASTER

Many of the symbols associated with Easter reflect an older past too. The Easter bunny was originally a hare, a sacred animal that is seldom eaten because of its association in Britain with the Goddess of Spring. (Horses are also holy and not eaten in Britain for much the same reason.) At this time hares are seen in the fields – it is the females who fight for territory and a mate.

Eggs, which are one of the main indicators of returning life at Easter, are fertility symbols in many lands. There are old customs where hard-boiled eggs are rolled down hills, or "shackled", that is shaken in a sieve, until only one remains unbroken, offering the owner a small prize. Now the chicken eggs are replaced with chocolate ones. Sometimes it is a round cheese, as a representative of the newborn Sun that is rolled down a hill and chased, or heated new pennies are thrown to the crowd as a gift from on high.

SPELL TO WELCOME THE POWER OF SPRING

With a shrine in your home, you can bring the benefits of each season into your house.

1 Pick some fresh spring flowers and catkins and place them before you. Focus on what you want to "spring open" in your life, ideally picking something that can be accomplished soon.

2 Hum a single long note of invitation and welcome, letting it resonate through you. Sing "Lady of Spring, Lady of Life, Lady of the Earth, Nature's Wife, reveal to me, in this season of birth, my way to .... I call you now."

3 Make a tube of your hands and breathe out or whistle to North then South then West and East. Sit still and listen for an answer. Keep the flowers in water where you can see them and before they have all died you will get your wish granted.

Feasts of Beltane, midsummer solstice and
Summer Rites

The days continue to lengthen as we move towards summer. As we follow Nature's course, this is the time to mark the burgeoning of life and the dominance of the Sun.

Beltane

Summer life in the country often begins with May Day, when the hawthorn, which is already green, is covered with its foaming white, sweet-scented flowers, which are sacred to the Goddess as spring bride. As the May blossomed, it was time to move cattle and sheep to the higher pastures and set about the tasks of summer. In the pagan year it is a time for Beltane Bonfires (Bel tan means "good fire"), when these were stoked with herbs and sacred plants so that the livestock could be purified by their scented smoke. Other fires burned on hilltops to strengthen the sun in his rising and bring fertility to the land, when the ashes were scattered upon it. The Goddess and the young God are wed in the hawthorn bower after a chase where she turns herself into a white hind and he hunts her and catches her. He is also the Green Man whose foliate face peers from the rafters of many churches all over Europe.

The Green Man is the sign of the verdant return of leaves and the springing power of grass and pasture. His presence in old churches is one that has never really been explained, for from his mouth come all kinds of holy plants, such as oak or hawthorn, ivy and artemesia, whose name shows that it is sacred to the Moon Goddess, Artemis. These are herbs of vision and farseeing, or they are trees whose leafing or fruit indicates an ancient festival. In a few churches, there are Green Women too.

Looking to Nature

In pre-literate times, festivals were set by what was happening in Nature and not according to some pre-ordained calendar date, as they might be now.

SUMMER RITUALS

At the high point of the sun there are other bonfire celebrations, where fires are lit on hilltops. In Cornwall, a ritual is enacted with words spoken in the ancient Kernow tongue of the land. Nine good herbs and nine useless weeds are tied in a bunch and a young woman, who represents the Goddess of the land, casts these into the flames, so that the good plants may increase and the weeds be destroyed.

Then doth the joyful feast of St John the Baptist take his turn
When bonfires great with lofty flame, in every town do burn,
And young men round with maids do dance in every street,
With garlands wrought of Motherwort, or the Vervaine sweet.

Thomas Kirchmeyer
"The Joyful Feast of St John" 16th century.

△ **Bonfires and torchlight mark midsummer.**

△ **May garlands celebrate summer's beginning.**

When groups of witches meet for a festival they often have to pick a weekend, but Nature is not so regular in her activities and it is worth really taking notice of what is going on in the gardens and woods around you. Rituals are often enactments of the story of the Goddess and the God, who having mated at the Spring Equinox, marry at Beltane, so that her Child of Promise may be born at midwinter. In the Middle Ages many brides were pregnant when they married, as it proved the couple's fertility and ensured a continuation of the bloodline. Some Beltane rites reflect this idea of the sacred wedding, or allow couples to renew their vows, often by jumping over the bonfire, or casting into it bunches of sacred herbs as a kind of sacrifice.

Many of these festivals began in pagan times as high points of the story of the Goddess of the Earth and her Lord, God of the Sky. Of course, this pattern, reflected in the growth of crops and the activities of animals, differs from place to place and country to country. If you don't grow corn you can't celebrate the death of the Corn King, and where vines aren't grown you can't have a vintage feast. You must look at your homeland and actually witness when the first blossoms of the hawthorn (May) are to be seen so that you can celebrate May Day.

△ **The countryside in full summer glory recognizes the power of the green Earth Mother and the bright Sky god.**

The Summer Solstice

The year continues to turn until mid-summer, the longest day and shortest night. and a time marked by the stones of many of Europe's most ancient monuments.

Academics and archaeologists have studied the alignments of these structures, once thought to have been put up by teams of skin-clad savages. Now they are recognizing the accuracy of the positions of the great stones, the complicated mathematics, and the sheer effort of shaping tough rocks with other stones and raising them in places where they have stood for 5,000 years. They have calculated how many man hours it would take to dig the ditches, haul the stones over huge distances by land or along rivers, and position them according to data that must have been collected and checked over many decades. Probably only the honour of great Gods and Goddesses would cause this amount of time and effort.

△ **Ears of corn ripen in warm sunshine, promising harvest and the reward of hard labour.**

SACRED DANCES

In England, summer is a time of Morris Dances. These involve troupes of mainly men dressed in white for the Goddess, with bells and ribbons; they dance the weather magic with hankies, and the ploughing, fertility magic with sticks, to the accompaniment of ancient tunes. Each team in lines dances in and out, like the tides of the sea, and their waving ribbons and bright costumes encourage the Sun to shine and the corn to grow green.

It is likely that women also had sacred dances, and perhaps the wives, grandmothers and daughters danced with sieves and baskets in the light of the Moon Goddess, to bring love and happiness, and joy within the home. These secret dances have been forgotten, while the men's daylight dances were preserved and are becoming ever more popular.

A SPELL TO DISCOVER THE GREEN MAN

The Green Man is one version of the old god of Nature who is at his height in Summer. He is protective and acts as a friend of animals and will help gardens to prosper. For this reason he is worshipped by some witches as Jack-in-the-Green or the Horned God, Pan or Cernunnos.

1 Weave a circle of bendy, leafy twigs and local wild flowers to make a garland, and place this on the ground around a jar containing a lit green candle. Sit beside it, facing South in an afternoon.

2 Sing "Green Man, unseen man, hiding in the trees, Old god of nature, Pan, move with the breeze. Show me or blow me a message from the green, Appear to me gently, I beg of you, please. Grant me the power of wild senses keen."

3 Sit absolutely still for as long as you can and if your spell is answered wild animals or birds, or other signs that Nature is listening will be shown to you.

4 When you finish, hang the garland on a tree branch as an offering, and say "Thank you green god, thank you old man, thank you Pan, lord of the wild things."

△ **Ancient peoples placed great stones to mark the passage of the Sun through the sky.**

Lammas, harvest, Michaelmas and the
Autumn Equinox

We now move on to the time of year when all the hard work of sowing and tending comes to fruition. It is time to gather in the crops ready for the hard winter. There are many ceremonies and rituals built around the harvest.

△ **Orchard fruits show how Mother Nature has bestowed her blessing.**

△ **The last sheaf of grain was cut in a ritual as it was thought to contain the living spirit of fertility.**

everyone had to join in the gathering, cutting the corn and binding it into sheaves. All kinds of other harvests would be gathered at this time of year as well, depending on where in the land people lived. Fish from the sea or rivers would be salted and preserved, as well as fruits and vegetables as their seasons came round. Before freezing, salting, drying and smoking were very important skills, and not without their magics too. Every kind of produce needed to keep for as long as possible so that the villagers would not suffer in the winter.

Harvests

As summer started to wane towards autumn, other harvests would be collected. In lands where vines grow, the grapes would be gathered and crushed to make a new season's wine, and olives were knocked from the trees. In other places traditional wines made from wild fruits and berries would be fermented. It has been said that if the Romans had not introduced wine made from grapes,

Lammas

After midsummer and the longest day, you have the start of the harvest, Lammas (Hlafmas or Loaf-mass from the Saxon, when the first new grain was baked into bread). Here the God as Spirit of the Corn becomes Lord of the Under/Otherworld, a place of magic and eternal youth, and corn dollies are made to keep his spirit of fertility until the spring sowing. Harvest to our ancestors was of great importance, for bread formed the basis of their diets, and if there was no corn they would actually starve.

Lammas could fall at any time from early July until late August for different harvests would ripen at different times, with crops of oats, barley and wheat being gathered as soon as they were ready. Barley was eaten as a grain, or fed to livestock, but more often it was malted and turned into beer as it is to this day. Because these grains were so important

△ **Women would gather together to spin and weave as the evenings drew in.**

Britons would always have drunk blackberry and elderberry wine as these plants, like grapes, have the wild yeasts on them that turn their juice into wine naturally.

Using Mushrooms

Mushrooms can provide food and medicine, as well as visions of the past and future.

There are a great number of mushrooms and other fungi that are edible, but you do need expert guidance to gather them safely. Fungi vary from the expensive truffles, traditionally hunted by dogs or pigs, to the common horse mushrooms and puffballs that are found in many places. Some of the poisonous toadstools are considered to have special properties.

△ If you know where to look, a wide variety of fungi can be found.

One of these is the fly agaric, the red and white mushroom shown in fairy tales. It is said that shamans in Lapland feed the mushrooms to reindeer to rid them of the toxic effects and then the shaman drink a potion made from the reindeer urine that brings visions of flight.

△ The low Sun of autumn fills a wood with the light and scents of the season.

△ The Archangel Michael, bringer of balance, shown here with his scales.

△ Falling leaves paint the landscape with golds and amber.

Michaelmas and the Autumn Equinox

The Autumn Equinox is when day and night are equal in length again, and the sun rises due East and sets due West. It is the entry into the sign of Libra the Scales, when dark and light balance. St Michael, or the Archangel Michael, is a bringer of balance because he overcame the forces of chaos and destruction. There are a great number of churches dedicated to Michael on the sites of ancient pagan temples, often on high hills or promontories. Many of these heights were dedicated to the Sun God and were places where people could get closest to the sky. There were sites of beacons and celebratory bonfires, and traces of stone circles or monoliths have been found on them.

Hallowe'en, Yule, Christmas, Twelfth Night –
Winter Customs

When the harvest is in and the Autumn Equinox and the Feast of St Michael have gone by, winter takes over, bringing with it cold days and long nights. Now is the time for reflecting on the past and future rebirth of spring.

Hallowe'en

The first festival of this season is the fire feast of Hallowe'en, Samhain. This takes place at the end of summer when all flocks, herds and family were gathered in from the cold and darkness. Hallowe'en is becoming a popular festival again, partly because it is at that dull time of year when summer has long gone and it is still a long time until Christmas.

Children enjoy the old Scottish custom of Trick or Treat, which migrated to America, and now is returning towards its British roots. Adults and children alike enjoy Hallowe'en parties where you can be a witch or ghost, the vampire or monster, and where games with apples, the fruits of the Celtic Tree of Immortality are played. People duck for them in buckets of water, eat them from strings, or cast the carefully pared skin over their shoulders to form an omen of the first letter of a special person's name. It is a way of appreciating this mystic fruit which, when cut in half crossways, shows the magical pentacle.

The Traditional Roots of Hallowe'en

Dressing up, Trick or Treat and many other games, involving bonfires and fireworks, can be traced right back to much older feasts and gatherings. Some of these ideas come into the way modern pagans celebrate this feast. In their calendar, it is the time when the Green Man or Lord of the Harvest departs into the otherworld, after his death in the corn field. The Goddess is in her third phase as Matriarch or Crone, when she is known for her wisdom, farseeing and magical powers. It is for this reason that Hallowe'en usually has some form of divination involved, either as a light-hearted party game, or more formally during a ritual. A Tarot reading for the year ahead could be examined in the Samhain circle, or those who could scry would stare into the dark glass to seek guidance and a new direction for the coming season.

In some old witch families, it was believed that the doors between the different worlds of people and their ancestors were open. At the Samhain feast a place was laid for the First Mother and First Father of the people, and those from other times could also join in. Not only were the forebears able to visit, but the souls of the children who would be born into the family or clan during the next cycle could come and meet their new parents. It is a time for speech, talking over the natural year that is ending, and planning for the cold months ahead. But it is also a time of silence, a time to listen to the old tales, told beside the hearth, or sung around a bonfire on a cold, frosty night, out under the stars.

THE HALLOWE'EN FEAST

Summer's end is marked by the first period of hard frost, usually at the beginning of November, and it was at this time that the excess sheep, cattle and pigs would be killed and salted down, so they didn't need to be fed when there was no grazing. This supplied the people with their meat for the winter, but the weather had to be cool or the meat would spoil before it could be smoked, salted or dried. Some parts of the creatures had to be eaten on the spot, and this gave rise to the Hallowe'en feast.

△ **Hallowe'en is a time of ghosts and legends, and making pumpkin lanterns and pies for the festival.**

△ **The Sun at midwinter symbolizes the beginning of the journey of the young Sun King.**

△ Midwinter celebrations counteract the dark nights with glittering decorations and an abundance of food and gifts.

Celebrating the Seasons

If you celebrate Yuletide and Twelfth Night – when the Mabon, the young Sun King sets out on his journey as champion of the Goddess – and either new or full Moons, you will have plenty of occasions for rituals incorporating part of the legend, or the symbols of each, as well as its aspects of magic. Each ancient festival has certain magical activities or powers associated with it, and if you devote a little time to getting to know the cycles of Nature, she will teach you her secrets. You need not dress your shrine differently for each festival – one way of dressing will be fitting for all.

△ Ice forms the cold heart of winter, when the pagan Gods sleep in their snowy caves.

Yule

December brings a collection of festivals celebrated by different people. There is the Winter Solstice on or around 21st December, when the longest night and shortest day occurs and some call this by its Saxon name of Yule. Yuletide is a time of feasting in winter, when the Yule Log, made of the root of a great oak tree or the Ashen Faggot, a bundle of sticks, from an ash tree, burns in the hearth for the 12 nights of the festival. It is lit from a piece of last year's log, and should be as big as possible. Today, as many houses don't have real fireplaces, the yule log is represented by a chocolate cake.

The pagan Yule is the time of the birth of the Star Child, the Mabon, the sacred Son of the Mother, Modron. He is the Child of Promise, whose coming brings hope to the wintry world. Like the birth of a real child, his coming is eagerly awaited within the ritual, and gifts of magical significance are offered to the young boy who may take his part in the Mystery Play of Mabon. His "mother" and "father" may be chosen when they eat the Yule cake, in which are hidden a dried pea and a dried bean, or two silver tokens that symbolize these. The cake is baked, marked across so one half is for the men and one half for the women. The ritual tells of the magic child's birth and as he ages one year for one day, by Twelfth Night he is old enough to earn his magical instruments and symbols, which are shown to the whole company, and their use and power are demonstrated. It can also be a time of initiation for other young people into the traditions of the clan.

Christmas

Christmas has its own traditions in the giving and receiving of presents, eating a special meal, and visiting relatives. Carols, which are now sung were originally dances. The story of the birth of Jesus and all its symbolism has links to far older sources. The tradition of a lit and decorated Christmas tree spread from Germany in the 19th century, but dressing up a tree with candles and ribbons in mid-winter is a very old tradition.

SPELL FOR THE TWELVE DAYS OF CHRISTMAS
Yule-tide or Christmas is a time of giving gifts. This is a spell to help you gain inner gifts by giving a small part of yourself each day for the Twelve Days.

1 Each day you will need to follow the same formula, lighting a large candle just while you chant the spell, and collecting a token which could be a sprig of Yule greenery, or a nut, or a Christmas tree ornament, to symbolise each day's spell.

2 At some time each day sing "Every day I gain life's gifts, and by this token, I'll repay, when it seems that good luck shifts, to others I'll give it away." Make twelve promises to be kept, one a month, throughout the coming year, which can be as simple as to speak kindly to a stranger or person who helps you, or to do a specific task which you know will help someone. You must not expect thanks or a reward, as this is to ask the inner world to repay when you need luck.

3 When you have made all twelve promises, one a day, put the ornaments somewhere safe for the months to come, and as you fulfil each promise you put away a token.

Understanding the turning wheel of time and
Meeting Our Ancestors

Every country has its own patterns of natural growth, of decay, rest and rebirth, and each land has had traditional celebrations at different times during this ever-turning wheel of seasons. If you wish to work magic, you will need to recognize and then connect to these currents and tides, because they give great power to ritual and magical work. There is no other way but to start to observe Nature, and everything that goes on around you. Notice the phases of the Moon, so that a mere glimpse of her in the sky tells you whether she is waxing or waning, and how far she is from being new or full. Get to know how the Sun rises and sets throughout the year, creeping along the horizon from midwinter to midsummer and back. Look at the clouds and learn to see them as harbingers of weather; become aware of birds and wild animals that are about even in urban areas. Get to really see things around you: plants developing in neighbourhood gardens or parks; crops in the fields; changes in the leaves of trees in woods; and every detail of the life around you wherever you are.

Perception

Only by becoming sensitive to what is really happening can you learn to sense inner things. It is no good trying to divine the future when you are totally blind to the present. By getting used to seeing the clues all around you everyday as to what is happening in the world, and then looking for those same clues in your scrying glass or Tarot pack, you will develop your psychic and perceptive powers. Notice the smallest changes in the lives of those around you so that you can sense their moods; record your dreams so that those aspects of your own hidden life are shown clearly to you. All these things take time and patience – no one else can give you these skills, or sell them to you, or initiate you into their use if you can't work at them yourself.

Meeting Our Ancestors

Every land has been inhabited and changed by its residents for thousands of years. When people first explored each region, they sought water, food, shelter and other materials from the landscape to make their lives possible. In many places they created or discovered areas they considered sacred, and began to construct ritual cycles, to encourage game for the pot, to find fruits and roots and herbs, or to help their cultivated plants thrive. Some painted wonderful scenes deeply hidden in caves, or decorated the walls of their shelters with magical images. They did their best to leave records, which now, even in our highly technical world, we cannot read. Yet there are messages there – instructions, spells, accounts and stories – set out in pictures, inscribed on stone, shaped into the landscape, yet written in languages that we can't yet decode. But they are our ancestors – their DNA and bloodlines run through us. If we use magic, we can travel back through the eons of time to meet them in the eternal land of dream, or in the magical realms which were real to them and can be explored by us. We have the same kinds of minds and bodies, the same fears and needs, perhaps the same religious beliefs and symbols. We can learn, through meditation and inner journeying, to return to the unspoiled land, by a river or ocean, to meet them and learn from them. More easily than ever before, we can examine their art and constructions, visit the places that mattered to them, see their tools and the things they made in museums, see their bones, watch new discoveries being uncovered by archaeologists and researchers.

However, we are unable to hear their songs, even though many of their musical instruments have survived and can be played. Their stories have been passed down to us

△ Great structures, such as this one in Mexico dedicated to the god Kulkulkan, have been built to rise up to the gods of the sky.

△ The great pyramids of Egypt can act as a link with our ancestors, as can other ancient monuments around the world.

△ **A horned Celtic god surrounded with forest creatures is depicted bringing gifts.**

via oral tradition, but the words and meanings have almost certainly changed along the way. To recover the original versions and hear them properly, we must reforge the ancient links that connect us to the first Goddesses of the land and recover the first arts of magic whose memories lie deep in our own. We have to go to these special places and ask the right questions.

Forging Links with Our Ancestors

When we light a real flame, it is as though it were a child of the original fires of our ancestors and of the ancient peoples of our lands. In the dark glass or the water, we may start to perceive the faces of the past, and when we celebrate the sunrises and moonsets, the equinoxes and solstices, and the passing phases of the Moon, we are joining directly to their perceptions too. As we begin to understand the power of the seasons and the tides of time which can heal and aid us in our own work, we are treading in the same footsteps that those old magicians, shamans and witches trod long ago. We can't prove an unbroken line of wisdom, but we can gently enter into a bond of love, honour and respect with the past and draw great strength from it.

AN INNER JOURNEY

Here is an inner journey to connect with your own ancestors or with the previous magical people of the land you inhabit.

1 Make your circle, and sit in the centre. Light only one candle at the centre and have about you flowers, very simple magical instruments made of wood, or bone or stone, a seashell for a cup and some spring water.

2 Allow the sacred space to form around you, so that you can feel the boundaries. This time it is a vessel able to take you back through time.

3 Relax and focus on returning to some seasonal feast of your ancestors, and allow the darkness to flow protectively around you. Become still and quiet.

4 See in that darkness a bonfire and begin to make out the shapes of people moving around it. Allow your inner sight to become clearer and show you greater details of who is there, and what they are doing.

5 Be at peace and watch the scene unfold around you. After a while you may find that you have shifted through time so that you are actually there, able to communicate and participate in what is going on.

6 Remain as aware as you can, smelling the air and woodsmoke, feeling the warmth of the fire, seeing the moving flames and the people about the fire. Acting with respect, see if you

can join in, seek help, and speak to these ancestors, whether they are your known family from a few generations back, or the oldest members of your nation or clan. Be there for as long as you feel comfortable.

7 When you sense that it is time to withdraw, offer thanks for their allowing you to be with them, and for any gifts or knowledge you have received. Slowly withdraw your awareness, back to your own sacred space, and contemplate the candle for a moment, detaching from the older fire.

8 If you have bread or fruit, eat some of them, pour the water into your shell and drink from it, in your mind sharing this simple communion with your forbears. Close the circle, but be willing to return on another occasion to explore the past further.

Karma past-life recall –
Reincarnation

The doctrine of reincarnation holds that each soul lives through many human lifetimes, gradually gaining skills and strengthening its power to evolve. An aspect of this divine spark is within everyone – it is immortal and does not die when our bodies do. We recognize this eternal factor within us and probably think of it as our "selfs". Just as the plants grow, blossom, fruit and die, so the human being grows, learns, reproduces, dies and is born again.

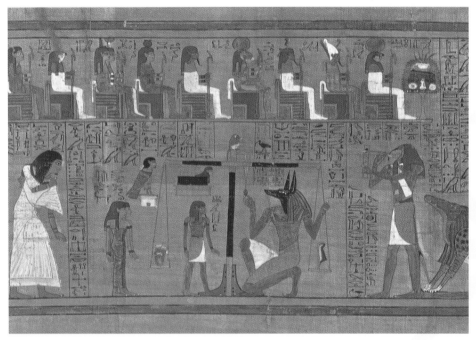

△ **In Ancient Egypt, the heart of the person that had just died was weighed by Anubis against the feathers of Maat, the goddess of truth.**

The Soul

As the soul lives each life on Earth, it gains new experiences and becomes more complete. Between lives it rests, in a state that might be thought of as "heaven". Here it can assess its own progress and is not "judged" or made to account for "sins" but can see dispassionately how it has done in life. If a certain part of its development has been overlooked, it will come back into life to learn the lessons so far omitted. This may account for geniuses, young children who can remember being someone else, and skills from earlier lives.

Karma

Central to the idea of reincarnation is the doctrine of karma, an Eastern term for which the Western world has no exact equivalent: it is a cyclical concept of action and reaction. Sometimes it is thought that it is simply a way for one individual to pay another back for harm done in a past lifetime, but it is far more complex than that. If you were killed by A in a past life and encounter him again in another incarnation, it does not mean that you have the right to kill A in order to get the balance right. Often there is some other way in which you and A work out the karma you share. Perhaps A can repay the debt in some other way, for A's death at this time might not be right. Sometimes it can be seen that your previous death was due, and that there was no blame. Without a great deal of digging it is hard to get to the bottom of a single event, as every life is affected by karma to a greater or lesser degree. It is the soul that chooses the conditions into which it will be born each time. No other being directs the pattern of reincarnation.

It is of course possible that long-lasting relationships can continue from one life to the next. It is important that the bonds of love should outlive the grave. If you can give out love, to God or to the Gods, to humankind, to those closely related to you as well as to casual acquaintances, it will be reflected back to you and you also will be loved. Be prepared to show love genuinely

A MIRROR SPELL TO SEE WHO YOU HAVE BEEN

This will allow you to get a small glimpse of the past, on which you can work to gain more details.

1 Make a magical circle of protection and calmness by sprinkling blessed water round you. Become relaxed and focused.

2 At night, place a mirror on a stand and a single lit white candle on a table so that the light shines on your face. Also take a sheet of writing paper and a pen. Write clearly, "I wish to see who I have been in a past life, at a time when all was going well. Reveal to me in this shining glass, I summon old 'me' by this powerful spell." Carefully burn the writing in the candle flame.

3 Just focus your vision on your eyes reflected in the mirror and after a while you may see the image change and become another face. It can seem a bit weird at first, but if you are patient and certain it is what you want, it will happen.

4 When your face returns to normal, say "Thank you, me, who ever you seem, perhaps we will meet again in a dream."

from the heart. Touch people lovingly, cuddle those closest to you, put your arm around someone in sympathy, support the elderly. Be open, unembarrassed and easy with those around you, and it will be repaid immediately by a happier, more loving atmosphere. There are a few who believe that crippling diseases are karmic debts being paid off, for individuals may have maimed, tortured or injured others in the past and have chosen to suffer for their cruelty. Or these individuals have chosen to come to Earth in imperfect bodies to learn hard lessons quickly, and so evolve. No one knows if this is true, but karma does teach lessons, and good and bad deeds may well be balanced out.

△ A universal symbol of rebirth, the legendary phoenix burns its own nest, and then is reborn from the ashes to live through another life.

Past-life Recall

If you do want to explore your own past lives, do go about it sensibly, because it can be an unsettling experience. It is vital to have a reliable companion, plenty of time, and to make detailed records. Do not take everything you learn for granted without checking the facts – there are plenty of accurate historical accounts of most times and places, and the research can help confirm whether what you recall is valid and "real", or just fantasy or imagination.

△ In many cultures, life after death is seen as going on in a beautiful sun-lit garden.

DISCOVERING YOUR PAST LIVES

One of the most effective ways to discover past lives by yourself is to develop an inner journey to the Hall of Records where you can locate your own personal Book of Lives and see there who you have been. This can avoid the emotional impact of re-living the past when undergoing hypnotic regression or some of the other new ways of accessing past-life recall.

1 Imagine very clearly entering an old building and climbing a staircase to a great library. There are a great number of books of all ages, sizes and types, and perhaps a more up-to-date section with other ways of data storage and retrieval.

2 Explore the place fully with all your senses, really "being there".

3 You will be guided by librarians who will be ready to help you find your own records. The volume of your lives will have your current name on it and it can be taken to a quiet corner of the library to study.

4 Continue to relax and allow whatever image of this personal record that will arise to do so, rather than dictating a particular form on it.

5 When you are focused, open the record and you are sure to find something of interest. It could be a family tree, written words in familiar or ancient languages, still pictures, or an image that is more like a window, through which you can pass to explore your own past.

6 Take as long as you need, deeply entering the experience but trying to remember as much detail of what you find as possible, for later research and consideration at the end of the session. You may experience life from the outside, merely witnessing domestic events as an onlooker, or you may find yourself reliving some past incarnation. What you get, and how deeply you are affected, will depend on how much you can go with the process. It is a learning curve, taken over a few sessions with time to consider and assimilate what you discover in between.

7 It is worth writing a report in your Book of Illumination or making drawings, and adding in anything you gain from research later on. Sharing the experience with a friend can be a great help.

△ Use the smoke from a snuffed candle to draw you into your meditation, then light the candle again afterwards to ground yourself in this world.

Developing the Super Senses

From ancient times, every worker of magic has had special skills. Some of these are inherited as a gift from the Gods or their ancestors; others have to be learned, just like any other skill. Most people are able to awaken these sleeping talents if they are willing to try.

Psychic powers mean

Minds Over Magic

Most magical arts are very serious and require hard work and dedication because they develop those hidden talents that everyone has but most people ignore. In the past, witches and magicians were set apart by the fact that they could heal the sick, foresee the future or discover water. Much magical training is aimed at developing these subtle senses and it is often a long, drawn-out process, for like expertise in sports, these skills take time to practise and perfect.

Sometimes this can seem very unrewarding, but there is a diverse range of other "supernatural" skills that you might never have considered. These can be valuable training techniques, or can even provide a variety of esoteric party games, which your friends can play and so demonstrate their possible psychic talents.

Psychic Games

It is worth trying some experiments in extra sensory perception (ESP), psychokinesis (PK, affecting material objects by "mind power"), and expanding psychic awareness. You and your magical companions, or perhaps a slightly wider group of your friends and family, for example, can get together to try out skills such as telepathy (conveying information from one mind to another), precognition or clairvoyance (guessing which card, for example, will be turned up next), or retrocognition (listing the order of an already shuffled pack of cards).

You may already have found that your magical interests have led to your getting "hunches" about doing, or not doing, certain things, or that hints and clues are found in dreams, or that you actually perceive bits of the future clearly in meditations or during divination sessions. Gradually, these psychic impressions will become clearer and easier to interpret, especially if you are able to devote some time in learning which skills you already have, and which need to be rehearsed.

So long as you have control over your ability to use psychic faculties you won't get into trouble, but if you allow yourself to relax your guard and become frightened by your sudden clairvoyance, or power seemingly to affect and change the future, you will need to watch out.

DEVELOPING YOUR PSYCHIC FACULTIES

If you have a pack of ordinary playing cards, you can begin some simple tests. Get someone to spread out the playing cards face down on a table and shuffle them very thoroughly, and then give you the whole deck, face down.

△ **Experiments in ESP can be done with ordinary playing cards.**

You then take this pack and, picking the cards up one at a time, still face down, try to guess, imagine or see what colour each one is. Place each card in turn, still face down, on one of two heaps, representing black and red.

PSYCHIC EXPERIMENTS

Parapsychologists working in laboratories with carefully selected subjects, using well-tested methods under strictly controlled conditions, have found that new subjects often score higher than those who had tried, and become bored with, card guessing, or attempts at bending metal. It was also found that a relaxed frame of mind was a help to "remote viewing" (astral travel to the magician).

If you get stuck with some cards, make another heap and go back to them at the end. When you have got to the end of the pack, turn over the heaps and see what has happened. You might be surprised how many you get right first go! Let a companion have a turn and see if they do better or worse.

In parapsychological research carried out in laboratories, experimenters use a pack of Zener cards, a set of 25 cards which have clear images of a circle, a cross, wavy lines, a square and a five-pointed star.

These are used for runs of experiments with people who claim psychic powers. Some have produced extraordinary results to begin with, but the scores tend to drop lower as boredom sets in. If you come across these Zener cards you might like to try some experiments with friends.

△ **Cards should be thoroughly shuffled at the start and conclusion of a practice session.**

PSYCHIC TAROT

Another experiment, which may be more interesting to magicians, uses Tarot cards. Place a pack face down across the floor or a large table and stir them about. The experimenter then picks up a card and, without seeing the picture, tries to name it, or describe the feelings, symbols or meaning of the card to a partner. Then both look at the card and see if any of it fits. Often, because the experimenter gets immediate feedback, by seeing the card after they have guessed, they will get better, accurate impressions.

△ **Open your mind and allow the images to come, then describe what you see.**

△ **The links between what you saw and what is there may not be immediately obvious.**

Taking Your Skills to a Higher Level

There are layers of interpretation attached to every Tarot card. These interpretations may be contradictory, depending on which of the 500 or so decks of Tarot cards you are using. In other words, your view of the cards may be linked to the symbolism of the card, or your own or a more traditional interpretation. This "game" has the added advantage of helping you to form telepathic links with your partner, as well as possibly discovering deeper levels of meaning to the Tarot, or any other system.

Later on, you may be able to send each other messages at a distance, at first by trying to get your friend to recognize a colour that you send at one o' clock, for example, and by identifying a simple shape received from her or him at two o'clock.

With practice, you might be able to send a number and a suit of playing or Tarot cards that would include a message, derived from the interpretation of that card or cards. Find out what sorts of information you can pass from mind to mind, starting with colours, plain shapes, numbers (either as the written figure, or a number of lines, dots or symbols, as that may be easier), and feelings such as energy, calm and so on. Use your own imagination to invent some suitable experiments to try. Each will help awaken, strengthen and control your psychic faculties.

An interesting method is to repeat the tests using a selection of picture postcards with clear images or designs. One person looks at the picture chosen at random from these and tries to convey the illustration to the receiver in another room. The receiver

enters a relaxed and meditative state, allowing the mind to be empty, and tries to sense what is being seen. Although it is not easy to be able to draw exactly the same picture, receptive people (as all magicians ought to be) should get some aspect of the design, or indicate the feeling of the sender's mind.

For example, if the card showed yachts sailing on a calm sea, with birds flying above, the receiver might draw triangles and say it felt windy, or sunny, or that there was a feeling of swaying, etc. Sometimes the emotion of a picture of lovers, or the scent of a flower, or the speed of racing cars can be sent more easily than the actual shapes, colours or minor details of the design. Match up the sender's and receiver's material, or allow the receiver to try and recognize the target in a selection of cards.

△ **Concentrate hard on the picture you hold in your hand and attempt to transmit the image to your partner.**

△ **After your partner has described the image received from you, study the card together and see how close you were.**

Learning to use divination –
The Tarot

Divination consists of a number of arts that use symbols, such as the Tarot cards, the I Ching hexagrams or a crystal ball to help you focus your clairvoyance or psychic vision on matters which may be occurring at a distance, or back and forth in time. There are a variety of different methods by which the doors to your own psychic abilities are awakened in a way which permits intuition to work. It is this "inner teaching" that may be thought to come from God or the Tarot Angel for example, which gives divination its name. By opening yourself gently to deeper awareness while using symbols, pictures or patterns from the various traditions, you gain an in-depth interpretation of them. This goes beyond repeating what might be written in a book.

The Tarot

Magicians and witches use a system of divination for looking into the future or for answering questions. The most popular is the Tarot, a pack of 78 picture cards whose symbolic meaning will need to be learned. There are several hundred designs available, some based on the original Marseilles deck, which has the 22 major arcana or trumps, as well as the four suits of 14 cards. In this ancient deck, the spot or playing cards are plain with coins, cups, swords and staves having only their numbers on.

Most modern Tarot decks have pictures on every card, and the best way to learn the meanings is to shuffle a new pack thoroughly and take one card each day. Place it somewhere you can see it and think what it seems to show, or meditate on the image. Write down your conclusions in a book kept for the purpose, and next day go on to another card, until you have examined all 78. You may simply focus on the name or number of the card, or try to decide what the picture shows at first, but gradually meanings will start to emerge.

Do not rush this learning process, as it will serve you all your life, and getting it to be meaningful is far more important than going through all the cards superficially. When you have discovered your own interpretations, return to the book of the deck and compare a guide book's views with your own, adding further notes to expand your personal book. Later you can expand the bare details by

△ **Every Tarot card has a wide spectrum of meanings according to various writers.**

reading other writers. Some of these may be scholarly, others light-hearted; some may be psychologically orientated, some personal or historical. In each case, the way that you interpret the symbols as they have turned up will vary with your own knowledge and the degree to which you are able to trust your own intuition in the matter. That, of course, is the key to an accurate and worthwhile reading. If your words only reflect some half-digested material gleaned from another's work, it will not show you the clear pictures, words or other information that will help

you pass on a good description of what may happen to your friend.

Practising Your Skill

Once you understand something about the symbols on the cards, begin each morning to ask a simple question such as "What kind of day will I have today?" and shuffle the pack, face down, then select three cards at random. See what they are and how you

A TAROT SPELL FOR INSIGHT
The Tarot is a powerful divination system. Use this spell each time you are doing a serious reading.

1 You will need a new Tarot deck and a square of silk, either red or bright blue, and a large surface with a clean flat cloth on it. Look carefully at each card, seeing the order in which they are placed. (If you are serious about Tarot Divination you will return the cards to this order when you have used them.) Place a tall, yellow or gold-coloured candle in a gold coloured holder and light it.

2 Place the Tarot cards face down on the cloth and, with both hands, mix them up very thoroughly, saying this spell: "Cards of wisdom, cards of grace, cards with magic on their face, open in me the holy power, to answer truly, at any hour. Open in me the skill of sight, to speak the truth by day and night. Let the knowledge in me rise, that all I speak is good and wise. Help me, Lord of the Tarot." Clap your hands three times over the cards.

3 Carefully select three cards and turn them over. These will show how well your spell has worked by their meanings. Collect up and sort the cards into suits and major arcana piles, then into order. Replace them in their box and wrap neatly in the silk to retain their power.

INTERPRETING THE SYMBOLS

Each divination symbol is really a reminder of some past event in a former life from which you can build a picture to convey to the querent who needs your help. The Tarot, for example, could be seen as the universal photo album. Everyone has pictures of their schooldays, their home, their first car, young loves, people they respect and so on.

These same ideas turn up in the Tarot, and in many other divination systems. When you explain a spread to the querent, you will have to recall that what actually happens to them won't be exactly the same as what you are remembering because that was a part of your own past, and the answer lies in their future.

△ **Study each card in turn as if it were a photograph, and work out its meaning for you.**

would interpret them in terms of your question. At the end of the day, see how they related to what happened. You will learn to ask better questions and start to understand the "language of the Tarot", and how it tries to answer. There are a great number of different spreads of cards, from a simple three-card quick answer to a basic question, to layouts with up to 56 cards giving an in-depth review of a problem in someone's life and what the next year holds in response to it.

The better you understand the messages of the cards, how they relate to time and how each suit is linked to areas of life, the more valuable a tool they become, but in the end, it is your intuition that will give you the answers.

Working with the Tarot

You can design Tarot rituals, or use the Aces to represent the Elements of Earth, Air, Fire and Water. These are usually Pentacles for Earth and money, Cups for Water and love. However, different authors give alternatives

for Swords, which used to be Fire, and Wands which used to be Air. Some writers prefer Swords for Air and Wands for Fire but you must decide for yourself. You can open a magical circle and call upon the Angel of the Tarot to help with divination, and you can work alone, or have your questioner or querent with you. Sometimes you may pick a card to represent the querent or the problem and, in many spreads, careful meditation will give far more valuable answers, so don't rush.

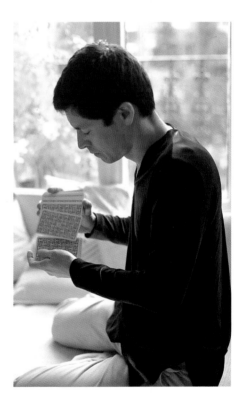

△ **To break the spell of a Tarot reading, shuffle the cards thoroughly afterwards.**

A WORD OF WARNING

This form of magical skill is usually used to help or advise another person and so it carries a heavy responsibility. No one wants advice from a clairvoyant who is wrong. Also, if you give advice to other people, their lives may be shaped by your words, and you take on the responsibility for giving good and accurate assistance to them. If you should misjudge a situation, you can bring unhappiness, distress or trouble to those you are aiming to help. It is a heavy burden, too often taken up without forethought or consideration of the implications of psychic counselling. If you tell people what to do, you get involved in their karma, and webs of commitment and attachment are woven between you.

Learning to use divination –
Scrying

The art of scrying, that is crystal-gazing or seeking pictures in a black mirror, a bowl of water or a pool of black ink, is another art that many magicians aim to master. It is best tried within a consecrated circle, which will banish those irritating psychic distractions that are present in everyday life.

△ **Some see swirling mists when they are scrying others will see the glass or crystal ball glow.**

Finding Your Relaxed State

To improve your success at scrying, it is necessary to be able to enter a deeply relaxed state at will, so performing this preparatory exercise might help with your scrying.

Find a time and place where you won't be disturbed for at least half an hour. You will need an upright chair and a notebook and pen for keeping a record – for example, a large "magical" diary in which you can enter visions or dreams and details of your progress at these exercises.

1 Sit upright with your feet flat on the floor or on a thick book so that your knees are at a right angle, and rest your hands comfortably. Close your eyes and relax.

2 Breathe out fully and then, counting at your own speed, breathe in for a count of

△ **Meditation outside frees your magic skills.**

YOUR ALTERED STATE OF CONSCIOUSNESS

Scrying is made harder by the fact that you have to reach an altered state of consciousness and then open your eyes. This is usually the sign to your subconscious that you are awake, so you come out of the state, back to normal awareness. There is a knack in holding a poised yet relaxed state and then allowing your eyes to open without disturbing it, which only comes after a bit of persistence.

Some people try too hard and get nothing; others give up after one or two failures, but if you do continue until it works, you will be rewarded by having another useful psychic skill at your command. Many novices find it quite easy and the images come naturally and clearly. It does help if you can remember your dreams, as scrying seems to use the same kinds of inner vision. Improve dream recall and scrying gets easier, or learn to crystal gaze and you will find you recall all your dreams.

four. Hold your breath for a count of four, breathe out for a count of four, then hold your breath out for another count of four.

3 Repeat this entire breathing cycle at least 10 times. If you lose count, it will be necessary to start again from the beginning. You may find this pattern difficult, in which case you can try a slower 10–5–10–5.

You can count quickly or slowly or, if you can feel your pulse while sitting in a relaxed position, count that.

4 Focus your whole attention on breathing rhythmically and relaxing physically. Gradually, you will find that this helps you to become calm and focused.

5 Bring your attention to the scrying glass, and gently open your eyes. You are in your relaxed state and ready to begin scrying.

Learning to Scry

Scrying is not a skill that you can learn automatically. It takes time, practice and concentration. You can learn to develop your ability to "see" by following these steps.

1 Allow yourself to sink into a relaxed state. Open your eyes to regard the glass, crystal, sphere or other "speculum".

2 Look within the glass, ignoring any reflections or points of light on its surface. Sink within it, forming the question in your mind. In a while, you will find that the glass seems to cloud over, or become dim. Through the mist, a dark patch may appear.

3 You might find yourself sinking into this dark patch, then pictures, signs, numbers, words or other symbols may appear before you. This will probably not happen in the first experiments you perform but will come with practice.

4 Continue for a number of regular sessions, allowing your companion to try in between times, and you will gradually master this ancient and very valuable skill.

△ **You can scry in a black mirror, candle flame or a bowl of water.**

Developing Your Scrying Skills

Divination is a knack, like balancing on a bicycle, or swimming. Once you can do it, practice brings you greater rewards and longer periods of concentration. Don't try too hard. Relax, and you will find words, images, still pictures or actions flitting past your point of awareness. Try to watch without attempting to grab hold of this material.

△ **It is much easier to get clear and valid images if you work within a magical circle of lights.**

After a while, you will find that the film show slows down, or the images or non-visual concepts remain visible long enough for you to study them. Like remembering dreams, you may need to tell yourself what is happening in order to fix it in your longer-term memory. It does get easier with practice.

You may find that it helps to cast a circle around yourself and the table with the speculum on it, or that to light a candle and some sweet incense will bring on a more psychic state of mind. Really it is a matter for patient experimentation to see what works best.

△ **Hold the crystal ball for a while to attune it.**

MAKING YOUR OWN SCRYING VESSEL

Because real crystal balls are rare, there are simpler methods you can try. One is to get a balloon-shaped wine glass and, using black enamel spray paint, spray the outside of the glass with several coats, allowing each to dry. Then you can gaze into the black bowl and see images in the same way as with a sphere. You can add some spring water if you find that helps, or just scry in a clear glass bowl of water.

You can also make a simple black "mirror" from a picture frame by replacing the picture with a sheet of really black paper.

1 You will need a picture frame, a piece of black paper and a pair of scissors. Take the frame apart and cut out a piece of paper to fit.

2 Place the paper in the frame so that it lies behind the glass.

3 Reassemble the frame and polish the glass thoroughly. Your scrying glass is now ready to use. Another way is to paint the back of the glass black.

Pendulums, Auras and Chakras –
Dowsing and Sensing

There are further ways of using your psychic senses for divination, such as dowsing, seeing auras and feeling chakras. All these skills can be used for healing minor ailments, so it is worth developing them as useful tools.

Dowsing with a pendulum

A skill every magician and witch should acquire is that of dowsing with a pendulum. It is a relatively straightforward skill, and a valuable one, as you can use it to choose remedies. Follow these simple steps:

1 Get a small, symmetrical weight and attach it to a piece of thin twine or cord.

2 Hold this over your other hand, held flat and palm up, and ask a basic question, such as "Is it Wednesday?" You will soon find the pendulum swings slightly, either in a straight line, or in a circle.

3 Command your inner self, which is causing the muscles in your hand to move, to work harder.

4 When you get clear movement, ask a question that has the opposite answer. Again your pendulum will swing in a different manner. Although some books say there is a definite swing for "Yes" and "No" it does vary from individual to individual. Also, you may find that if you ask questions about another person, or someone of the opposite sex, the swings change their movement.

5 Keep on practising until you can get firm, accurate and consistent results from this experiment, as it has many magical applications.

6 Keep on trying until you are sure you can understand the code your own pendulum is using under different circumstances, and then you can test it on healing situations.

Dowsing to Heal

You can experiment with lists of herbs, massage oils, Bach remedies or forms of treatment with which you have become competent so that you can dowse along the list, picking out things to try in a particular case. You may need a sample from the sick person; a clipping of hair or nails, or a drop of saliva on a clean tissue will be sufficient to link you together while you investigate. If

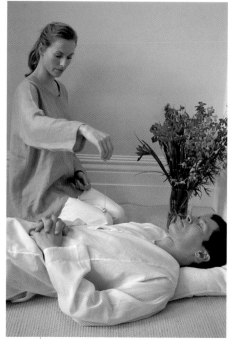

△ **You can use a pendulum to sense the energies around a person's aura and judge their health.**

they are present, you can ask questions while swinging the pendulum over their hands, or you might feel more confident if they supply the sample and allow you to work on their problem by yourself. Always be sure that you are dealing with an ailment you can handle, and if you are in any doubt, insist that your patient gets proper medical advice.

△ **Hold the pendulum loosely by a length of thread and allow it to swing freely.**

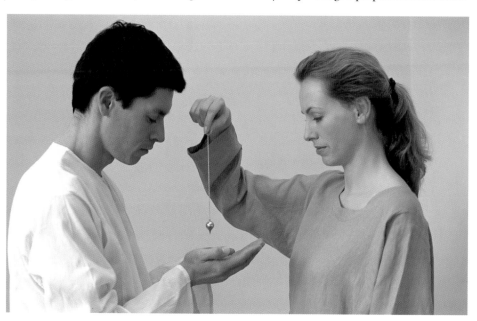

△ **When you have established a code of swings, you can ask a series of questions over your partner's hand.**

△ **A traditional dowsing rod is made of hazel and held in this rather awkward grip**.

Auras

You can use a pendulum to discover the edge of someone's aura. Start about 10 m (30 ft) away from them and walk towards them, stopping every pace and testing by asking the question "Does the aura reach here?"

Of course, it is much more useful to be able to see auras, and this is a skill that can be learned with patience. Ideally, you should look at another person standing in front of a plain, pale surface. If this is your friend, ask them to sway slightly from side to side while you stand about 5 m (15 ft) away, looking at the edge of them. After a while, you will see

a light colour which moves as they do. With practice over a number of sessions, you will start to be aware of layers of lighter or deeper tone surrounding them. This is usually a series of bands, starting close to their body with the etheric, which is a dense, pale, smoke-coloured layer a few centimetres or inches wide. Beyond that, stretching some distance, are a number of bands of what you will come to see as varied shades, going all around their outline, and in front of them too. You can try half-closing your eyes so that you are seeing through your eyelashes – some people find this helps. The aura is constructed of rays of light, and to get an idea of what it looks like, squint at a candle flame. You may well see a kind of radiating rainbow of light around the centre. This is what an aura looks like, and it is a matter of time and practice before you can identify the bands, and eventually the separate colours. Some of these are beyond normal vision and may be hard to name or identify.

Interpreting Auras

There are numerous books on interpreting the colours of auras, as to state of health, mood and so on, but you should know that you are looking through your own aura so the colours are a combination and may seem murky. You can see your own aura by standing naked in front of a mirror in a dimly lit room, and gazing with your eyes unfocused at your reflection. The colours of the outer aura will be changing all the time, varying with emotion, hunger and temper,

THE THREE LAYERS OF AN AURA

Most people's auras basically have three layers.

The inner etheric is easily visible to ordinary eyesight in a dimly lit room as a smoky band outlining the figure, and is seen best against naked flesh.

Beyond that is a wider band of the astral health region, seen as faint-coloured filaments, such as you sometimes see around power lines on misty days.

Outside that is an even fainter layer, the fine threads of the emotional aura, which connects to all the people, places and objects with which you have any link.

as well as general state of health, alertness and concentration on other people, which will brighten the filaments of auric material by which you are linked to them. Each individual's aura is different, and interpreting a healthy or unhealthy aura is entirely dependent upon the individual and the intuition of the viewer.

It may well be that it is along these delicate threads that the shared thoughts of telepathy flow; when you are psychometrizing an object (sensing its history by touch), the impressions you receive are obtained from the same source.

Sensing Chakras

Within everyone's aura are the chakras, a series of seven energy centres that run right through us. The base chakra is red and centred in the sexual region. It rules raw emotion.

Next is an orange sphere in the belly, dealing with absorption and elimination, both physically and psychically. Above that at the solar plexus is a golden yellow chakra, our Sun and self centre. In the chest is the emerald green heart chakra, for love and harmony. At the throat is a brilliant blue flower of living light, our power of communication and speech. At the forehead is a violet purple chakra linking to our intelligence and wisdom. At the top of the head is a brilliant white chakra of light which connects us to the Creative Spirit, through which religious feelings flow in and out.

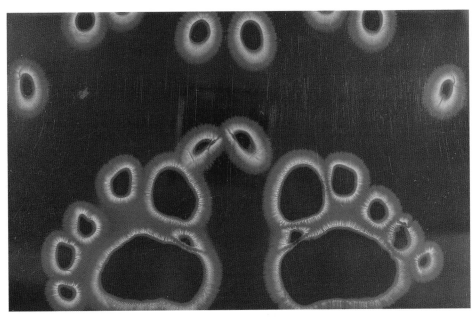

△ **Kirlian photographs show the aura around living things.**

The unseen forces that help us to

Learn From Inner Teachers

The occult arts have always recognized the reality of the "unseen forces" that may help and heal, instruct and guide. Magicians or witches do not usually call up the spirits of dead people, accepting, on the whole, that the immortal human spirit needs to rest and assess its past life before being brought back into incarnation – it doesn't want to be goaded by friends or relatives who are still alive into giving an account of its activities after it has cast off its mortal body. Nor will it necessarily have instantly gained profound wisdom, thus being able to answer all the questions that still beset those remaining in the "vale of tears". Certainly there are discarnate sources of knowledge that may be contacted through magical applications of some of the spiritualists' methods, but magicians or witches generally prefer to use their own ways to receive information from hidden masters or inner guides.

A Word of Warning

It is wisest not to attempt trances or try to contact discarnate spirits unless you have a reputable teacher, or expert help is at hand. There are lots of safe and more rewarding experiments you can try, and when you have fully mastered many of the occult skills then, if you are still interested, you may attempt more advanced journeys into the unknown regions.

Meeting Inner Teachers

Magicians and witches may have the ability to talk to teachers of wisdom from the past, or their own ancestors, or the people who founded their tradition, but this is done by creating an inner journey to the place in which these wise beings would dwell, and going there to hear what they have to say. All the time, the modern magic worker is in control and able to terminate the experience if necessary.

Inner Plane Adepti

Some schools of magic do have named inner teachers who are known as the Inner Plane Adepti or Hidden Masters of Wisdom. These great instructors may have been famous living people or they may be Angels who have never lived on earth.

A well-established magical lodge will have one or more of these teachers, who are invited to witness the workings of the magi-

△ **Machu Picchu is an ancient sacred site dedicated to the Sun**.

cal order and give guidance or instruction as necessary. If a group is fully aware of its Inner Plane Adept, they may see him or her during group meditations, or one member of the group will have the skill to perceive this inner teacher and convey their words or philosophy to the other members. It requires a lot of faith and trust to enter a mind-to-mind contact with some unseen being, but those who are experienced in this method gain a great deal of genuine and original teaching material.

The Unseen

Other unseen beings who are important to many branches of magic are the Angels and Archangels who have many functions, as healers, teachers, protectors and illuminators of humanity. Working with Angels is very popular because they appear to be benevolent beings of light, and are found in many religious philosophies. Pictures from Ancient Egyptian temples show winged goddesses who have many of the qualities of Angels, and Christians, Muslims, Jews and many other faiths have accounts of Angels in their religious texts.

There are many different kinds of Angels, who are particularly important to followers of the Hebrew mystical system of the Qabalah. The central glyph of this philosophy is the Tree of Life, which has ten spheres of creation. These are commonly linked to the powers of the planets, but each sphere also has an Angel who rules over its working in the Earth plane.

△ **The Temple at Delphi was one of the most powerful oracles of the ancient world**.

△ **Many people believe that cemeteries are haunted by the ghosts of the dead**.

△ **By meditating on the power of light, you may be able to call forth a vision of an Angel.**

Angels, whose name means, "messenger" in Greek, are thought of as the active hands of the Creator. They have no free will and travel between Earth and Heaven, bringing news or offering assistance. You could see them as God's robots, but they are powerful none the less. The Archangels of the Qabalah are concerned with the planets according to this list:

For Earth there is Sandalphon
For the Moon, Gabriel
Mercury has Raphael
Venus has Hanael
The Sun has Michael
Mars has Samael
Jupiter has Sachiel
For Saturn there is Cassiel

Each of these angels has a colour and particular task allotted to him, which he will work to fulfil in conjunction with humanity.

Meeting Angels

Angels may be called upon by lighting a candle, relaxing and asking them to appear, or they might offer help to you, if you genuinely need their assistance. They don't always look like the familiar pictures seen on Christmas cards, as they can be vast in size, and as subtle as auric light. Sometimes you see them as huge, delicate cloud formations like wings or feathers blown by the wind, and tipped with sunlight. They are always beautiful, and if you find yourself in their presence, it can be emotionally very moving.

△ **The white lady is a common form of haunting found in old houses and the countryside.**

△ **An artist's impression of the interior of the Delphic oracle, and with consultation in progress.**

GUARDIAN ANGELS

Everyone has a personal Holy Guardian Angel, whom you may have encountered if you have been seriously ill or had an accident, for they come to save and protect you. There is even a lengthy magical process called the Rite of Abramelin, by which a magician spends six months in prayer and concentration in a secluded place, after building an altar, mixing special incense. He can then focus on meeting his Holy Guardian Angel.

A WORD OF WARNING

Sadly, some people who have taken part in séances, played at "raising ghosts" or light-heartedly dabbled with Ouija boards have scared themselves. A few have opened doors to psychic perceptions that they did not know how to close, or attracted the attention of entities that they could not control, but if you are aspiring to master the skills of magic, you ought to know what you are doing. Remember that you are in control, and though you may encounter surprising things during your magical training, none can harm you unless you lose your nerve, or give them entry to your inner mind. So long as you work in the power of light, act sensibly and treat all beings – be they Gods, Angels, ghosts or Elementals – with respect, you will gain a great deal from your experiences.

The power of the mind for
Blessing and Protecting

Blessing is an essential art in the witch's or magician's set of skills. We have looked at self-blessing, but sometimes you may also need to bless places. You may sometimes have felt, when entering a place, that the atmosphere was wrong or, when moving somewhere new, that it was still disturbed by the previous occupants. Performing a blessing can change this and put the atmosphere right for you, or others.

△ **A staff may be used to create a protective circle.**

△ **A large number of candles placed in the corners of a room will move on stagnant energies.**

Blessing Yourself or Another

Often, before dealing with a difficult situation, or if you need healing, or if you want to work some powerful magical ritual, you might find the following exercise very helpful.

Work through it quite slowly, really feeling the colours, or seeing the flowers, and sensing the different energies. By doing this exercise, and imagining a set of rising colours up your body, you can become filled with this health-giving chakra power.

1 Stand comfortably upright and close your eyes. Imagine that you are standing on a dark, black, curved surface. It is so intensely black that you could almost imagine it is the night sky, spangled with brilliant stars. Moving up your body from your feet, the colour changes to a dark, peaty brown, fading gradually as you move up your legs to a russet brown.

2 At the top of your legs, the colour is crimson red. Above that is a band of orange across your stomach fading into a yellow band in the region of your solar plexus. Above the yellow, the colour changes to a rich leaf green over the heart region. At the top of your chest and throat, the colour changes through turquoise to a brilliant blue at the Adam's apple. From the bright blue, the colour changes to deep violet on the level of your third eye, in the centre of your forehead, and finally there is a change to a brilliant diamond whiteness at the top of your head.

3 Allow these colours to become vivid and definite and try to discover a gradation of tone, from very dark at the feet to a brilliant-white light above the top of your head.

See the most vivid and shining whiteness as a great ball above your head and then imagine drawing this force downwards through each colour band. It comes from beyond you, for it is the healing power of the creative force, or perhaps one of the healing Angels.

5 As the light flows down through you, sense it opening up a centre of protecting and balancing force, like a rose unfolding. The chakra at the crown of your head is the link with your "Higher Self", through which you may work magic.

△ Exorcists have used words from a sacred book, the sound of a bell and the light of a candle to drive out harm.

CHANGING THE ATMOSPHERE
A common problem is when someone moves into a new home they feel disturbed by the atmosphere left behind by the previous occupants. You can deal with this matter fairly easily, if you are just changing the atmosphere to suit the new tenant, not trying to shift a real ghost or haunting – that is a job for the experts.

1 Bless yourself and the house occupant as described to the left.

2 Carry a twig of rowan wood bound with a red thread or ribbon around the whole dwelling sunwise in every room and space, from attic to basement, sweeping out any old energies and atmospheres.

3 Sweep these out of the front door as if they were dust.

4 Go outside, light a new white candle and carry it in. Carry the candle around all the rooms and spaces, sunwise, seeing bright, new light entering.

△ Establish a small altar or shrine in the corner of your house to honour the Elements.

What the Colours Mean

At the forehead is a blossom of intense violet purple, which represents your psychic faculty.

At the throat, as the brilliance flows downwards through your body, there flowers the blue rose of communication and speech.

Below that there is a strange green flower at the heart centre, through which the power of love and compassion flows out to others.

Below that is the main healing centre of the solar plexus, through which the magical life force of the universe may be directed, in rays of Sun-golden light, to those in need.

Across your abdomen is an area of digestion and the orange-coloured flower that helps you cope with the mundane aspects of healing the sick, and will assist indigestion.

Below that is the crimson blossom filled with the brilliance of white light that enlivens your most basic urges of sex and true unity. This can be used to heal and balance your own life but it cannot pass out a healing power to others until you have fully mastered the technique of opening and controlling this centre of energy.

Below that is a darker region of stability and strength. It is the strong base on which the blossoms of sacred light grow. This is a mysterious firmament, which is why it may be envisioned as sprinkled with stars. Perform this exercise to feel balanced, protected and able to deal with problems.

Psychic Upsets

Many psychic upsets are the result of playing with inner matters, such as using a Ouija board, trying to work strange rituals, or attempting to set up a séance without knowing how. These things can open a crack between the ordinary self and the inner one. If people have fears or phobias, or repressed memories, these will be the first through the gap. In the hands of trained witches and magicians, some of these methods of contacting the inner self are valid and safe but they can be extremely dangerous.

5 When all feels well, you can recite this Navajo blessing:

This home will be a blessed home.
It will become the house of dawn.
Dawn light will live in beauty in it.
It will be a home of white corn,
It will be a home of soft goods,
It will be a home of crystal water,
It will be a home dusted with pollen,
It will be a home of life-long happiness,
It will be a home with beauty above it,
It will be a home with beauty all around it.

End Word
Table of Correspondences

The subjects of magic and witchcraft are vast and ancient. Here it has only been possible to show a few glimpses of this fascinating subject. If you are willing to master the gentle arts of meditation and inner journeying, dip into the symbolism and explore the many subjects that are set out here, you will gain a number of valuable skills whose roots may lie in the ancient wisdom of your land, but whose uses are always contemporary. None of these subjects is easy, nor are they matters that can be learned in a few moments, but the basic information given here ought to guide you onward safely and surely.

The many beautiful and evocative pictures in this book present a whole study in themselves. Meditate on each, trying to discover what it shows. Constructing the symbols, instruments and equipment will allow you

to reach powerful states of awareness. Magical skills include the abilities to see into the future and to work with healing, ritual and talismans, but it is also the skill to make wine, to bake bread, to carve and paint and draw and design. Poetic inspiration is magical; so are the arts of writing rituals, arranging flowers, constructing shrines and watching the Moon. If you become more aware of the world around you and

its seasons, you will see reflections of those changes in your own life, and change is magic.

If you find that your horizons are widening, that you are seeking a new spiritual alignment, that can only be good. Perhaps you will be drawn to the cycles of ancient seasonal festivals, and want to celebrate them. Maybe ancient arts will speak to you, be they story-telling, song, chants, dance or ritual. These are all gifts from the Great Mother, the first Goddess, in whose lap we dwell, and from whose bounty we have our nourishment and support. There are no rules except to seek understanding and be the best human being you can, sharing love, light, life and healing with all around you, and with our home on this blue-green jewel of a planet, floating in space. Remember, we are all Earth's children, but our destiny is beyond the stars. (MG)

TABLE OF PLANETS

PLANET	MOON	MARS	MERCURY	JUPITER	VENUS	SATURN	SUN	EARTH
Day	Monday	Tuesday	Wednesday	Thursday	Friday	Saturday	Sunday	Any
Metal	Silver	Iron	Quicksilver	Tin	Copper	Lead	Gold	Any
Colour	White	Red	Orange	Royal Blue	Green	Black	Yellow	All
Gemstones	Moonstone Pearl	Garnet Bloodstone	Opal Beryl	Amethyst Lapis Lazuli	Emerald Peridot	Jet Onyx	Diamond Amber	Agate All semi-precious stones
Incense	Jasmine	Tobacco	Mastic	Cedar	Rose	Myrrh	Frankincense	Dittany of Crete

GODS AND GODDESSES FROM THE VARIOUS PANTHEONS

Greek	Artemis	Ares	Hermes	Zeus	Aphrodite	Chronos	Helios	Gaia
Roman	Luna	Mars	Mercury	Jupiter	Venus	Saturn	Sol	Ceres
Angel	Gabriel	Samael	Raphael	Sachiel	Hanael	Cassiel	Michael	Sandalphon
Number	9	5	8	4	7	3	6	10

Table of the Elements

Tables of correspondences are an important part of the magic worker's tools. There are many available that will be vital as you start on your magical journey, but once you have become more experienced you will find the confidence to add your own information.

DIRECTION	EAST	SOUTH	WEST	NORTH
Time of Day	Dawn	Noon	Sunset	Midnight
Season	Spring	Summer	Autumn	Winter
Element	Air	Fire	Water	Earth
Magical Instrument	Wand	Sword/Dagger	Cup	Pentacle/Stone
Altar Symbol	Incense	Lamp	Chalice	Platter
Communion Symbol	Scent	Heat	Wine/Water	Bread/Salt
Elemental Symbol	🜁	🜂	🜄	🜃
Archangel	Raphael	Michael	Gabriel	Uriel
Human Sense	Hearing/Smelling	Sight	Taste	Touch
Art Forms	Poetry/Painting	Dance/Drama	Music/Song	Sculpture/Embroidery
Creatures	Birds/Bats	Salamanders/Lizards	Fish/Whales	Domestic Animals
Elemental Beings	Sylphs	Salamanders	Undines	Gnomes
Polarity	Male positive	Male negative	Female negative	Female positive
Exhortation	To Will	To Dare	To Know	To Keep Silent
Greek Wind God	Eurus	Notus	Zephyrus	Boreas
Musical Instruments	Wind Instruments/Harp	Brass Instruments	Strings/Bells	Drums/Percussion
Colours	Gold/White	Scarlet/Red	Blue/Green	Black/Deep Green
Mythical Beast	Winged Horse	Dragon	Sea serpent	Unicorn
Magical Arts	Divinations	Ritual	Healing	Talismans
God Forms	Sky/Weather God	Sun/Protector God	Moon/Water Goddess	Earth/Underworld Goddess
Meditation	Sky/Clouds	Bonfires	The Ocean/Rivers	Fertile Landscape
Images and Themes	Mountain Tops	Flames	Lakes/Pools	Caves/Rocks
	Flying	Volcanoes	Living under Water	Growing Organically
	Sunrise	Walking through Fire	Setting Sun	Moon/Stars/Night
	Wisdom & Knowledge	Sun at Noon	Healing and Calm	Growth and Life

Book List

94

Book List

It is impossible to print a comprehensive book list because there are so many titles that a witch or magician should read, both modern texts on magical arts and books on occult history.

Most of these authors have written additional books to those listed.

Robert Bauval & Adrian Gilbert
The Orion Mystery
Heinemann

Robert Bauval & Graham Hancock
Fingerprints of The Gods
Mandarin, UK

W.E. Butler
Magic and The Magician
Aquarian Press, UK

W.E. Butler
Lords of Light
Destiny Books, USA

Chic & Tabitha Cicero
Self-initiation Into The Golden Dawn Tradition
Llewellyn, USA

Vivienne Crowley
Living As A Pagan In 21st Century
Thorsons, UK

Gustave Davidson
A Dictionary Of Angels
Free Press/Macmillan, USA

Melita Denning & Osborne Phillips
Foundations Of High Magic
Llewellyn, USA

Melita Denning & Osborne Phillips
Planetary Magic
Weiser, USA

Janet & Stewart Farrar
Eight Sabbats For Witches
Hale, UK

Janet & Stewart Farrar
What Witches Do
Hale, UK

Charles Fielding
The Practical Qabalah
Weiser, USA

Charles Fielding
The Story Of Dion Fortune
Thoth, UK

Dion Fortune
Sane Occultism
Aquarian, UK

Dion Fortune
Applied Magic
Aquarian, UK

Dion Fortune
The Mystical Qabalah
Aquarian, UK

Dion Fortune
The Secrets Of Dr. Taverner
Aquarian, UK

Dion Fortune
The Magical Battle Of Britain
Golden Gates Press, UK

Dion Fortune/Gareth Knight
The Circuit Of Force
Thoth, UK

Dion Fortune/Gareth Knight
Introduction To Ritual Magic
Thoth, UK

R.A. Gilbert
Revelations Of The Golden Dawn
Quantum, UK

David Goddard
The Sacred Magic Of The Angels
Weiser, USA

David Goddard
The Tower Of Alchemy
Weiser, USA

W.G. Gray
Magical Ritual Methods
Weiser, USA

Marian Green
Practical Techniques Of Modern Magic
Thoth, UK

Marian Green
The Path Through The Labyrinth
Thoth, UK

Marian Green
Everyday Magic
Aquarian/Thorsons, UK

Marian Green
A Witch Alone
Thorsons, UK

Gareth Knight
A History Of White Magic
Mowbrays, UK

Caitlin & John Matthews
The Western Way
Arkana/RKP, UK

Israel Regardie
The Golden Dawn
Llewellyn, USA

R.J. Stewart
The Underworld Initiation
Aquarian, UK

R.J. Stewart
Advanced Magical Arts
Element Books, UK

Doreen Valiente
The Rebirth Of Witchcraft
Hale, UK

Doreen Valiente
The Abc Of Witchcraft, Ancient And Modern
Hale, UK

Doreen Valiente
Natural Magic
Hale, UK

Tony Willis
Magick And The Tarot
Aquarian, UK /Sterling, USA

Colin Wilson
Atlantis To The Sphinx
Virgin Books, UK

For light reading, there are numerous Fantasy and Sci-fi writers whose books have magical themes, or who are witches or magicians themselves. These writers include: Charles de Lint, Umberto Eco, Robert Holdstock, Katherine Kurtz (Adept Series), Terry Pratchett (Discworld Series) Robert Rankin, Charles Williams and Marion Zimmer Bradley.

Glossary

Agape (pronounced A-gar-pey) Greek for a love-feast, which developed into a communion meal.

Age of Aquarius Due to the movement of the Sun compared to the Earth against the stars, we are entering the Age of Aquarius, when these stars rise at dawn on the Spring Equinox.

Age of Pisces At present the Sun rises against the stars of Pisces at the Spring equinox, as it has done for about 2,000 years.

Amulet An object, often in the shape of an eye, worn to ward off harm.

Astral Travel Spiritual journeys, often during sleep, when the dreaming self leaves the physical body. Sometimes called "out of the body experiences".

Athame (pronounced Ath-a-mey) A ritual dagger used by wiccans.

Aura The energy patterns around living things, visible to witches and magicians.

Beltane An old bonfire festival at the beginning of May, when the hawthorn (May) flowers. The name is derived from the Celtic words "Bel", good or god, and "tan", fire.

Book of Illumination A personal record of spells, poems, rituals and other useful information collected by the magic worker.

Book of Lives Also known as the Akashic Record, it is a living archive in which all a person's lives are detailed.

Book of Shadows A book written by each wiccan, copying the rituals and festivals of their particular coven or line of initiation.

Ceremonial Magician Male or female, of any religious tradition, a ceremonial magician's knowledge is more philosophical and intellectual than it is religious. The different, ancient traditions of the Western Mysteries are important.

Chafing Dish A flat dish on which incense is burned on charcoal.

Chakra Sanskrit for "wheel", it is one of seven energy centres running through the body.

Coven A group of thirteen or fewer wiccans, led by a High Priestess and High Priest. It derives from the same word as "convent".

Deocil Clockwise or "godwise", this is the direction the Sun appears to move in the sky.

Discarnate Not alive on Earth, as ghosts or angels.

Divination The many arts of consulting the "divinity", reading Tarot cards, seeking water or consulting oracles.

Dowsing From the old Cornish, "to seek", especially water or buried treasure, using a Y-shaped hazel dowsing wand.

Ephemeris This is a list of tables of positions of the planets, the Sun and Moon, used by astrologers.

Equinox The time of year when day and night are equal.

Esbat A meeting of wiccans, at the full moon usually. It derives from the old French "esbattre", to dance.

Glyph A magical diagram.

Golden Dawn The Hermetic Order of the Golden Dawn was founded in 1887, in England. Many modern magical impulses have arisen from this, including the use of the Tarot for divination and pentacles for protection.

Golden Mean This is a ratio between the lengths of the sides of a rectangle which produce regular patterns. It occurs in nature in spiral snail shells and flower petals.

Hall of Records The repository for the Books of Lives.

Hermetic Mysteries Hermes was the Greek God of wisdom, based on the Egyptian God, Thoth, who gave the understanding of magic to humankind. Mysteries are things which cannot be told, only experienced.

Holy or Holey Stones These are stones, sometimes fossil sponges, which have natural holes right through them. For hundreds of years they have been hung by red wool or ribbon to bring luck.

Imbolc A festival in early February when ewes lamb. Imbolc means "ewe's milk" in a Celtic tongue. The festival is also called Candlemas or the Feast of St Bride.

Inner Plane Adepti These are otherworldly teachers: some are discarnate wise people; others are angels.

Karma A Sanskrit word for fate or balance. Every action accrues spiritual profit or loss, and through a series of reincarnated lives, the balance must be worked out.

Key of Solomon This is a book from the Middle Ages which sets out how talismans are to be made and which symbols should be used, and gives the basis of some rituals.

Lodge A group of magicians meet in a lodge, as do Freemasons. It is a term used for both the building or temple and the group itself.

Mabon In Welsh this means "son" or "boy" and is another name for the divine child born at midwinter.

Menses A woman's "moon flow" or period.

Pentacle A five-sided shape ("penta" is Greek for five); as opposed to a pentagram, which has five points.

Psychometrize To sense by touch the history of an object or information about its owner.

Qabalah One of the three spellings for an ancient Hebrew system of philosophy, wisdom and magic. These are the Jewish Kabbalah, the Christian Cabala and the mystical Qabalah. The variations come from transliterating the Hebrew letters QBL into English.

Querent In a divination situation, the querent is the one asking a question that the diviner is trying to answer.

Rite of Abramelin This is a six-month-long magical retreat aimed at establishing communication with a Holy Guardian Angel.

Rosicrucian Tradition Based on the writings of a secret 16th-century brotherhood, whose symbol was a rose and a cross, this is a series of rituals, healing arts and magical skills. Partly preserved by the Freemasons and partly by alchemists and magicians, its roots go back to Ancient Egypt.

Sabbat Derived from "Sabbath", the holy day of the week, these are the eight important seasonal festivals of the wiccans.

Scry Derived from the French "descrier", to proclaim, scrying means divining by crystal-gazing. A scrying glass is a crystal ball.

Shaman Originally one from a tribe in Siberia in Russia, who worked with magic and spirits. Having experienced death, a shaman can recall the souls of the sick.

Sidereal Star time, used by many astrologers as the time frame from which they calculate the positions of the planets and stars in a horoscope. It differs slightly from "clock" time.

Skyclad Some wiccans work their rituals naked or "skyclad". It refers to when they met out of doors.

Solstice At midsummer and midwinter the Sun reaches its highest and lowest points of its cycle, giving each hemisphere of the world its shortening and lengthening days.

Speculum A speculum is any kind of gazing glass or scrying ball, such as a crystal ball or black mirror. It is used to see into the future or from a distance.

Sunwise Clockwise. To open a ritual space, it is usual to walk circles clockwise, sunwise or deocil. Close the circle or space by walking anticlockwise.

Talisman A deliberately-made object which draws on the power and symbols of the planets or signs of the zodiac, often using archaic writing, to bring about a single specific purpose.

Thurible An incense burner, often on chains so it can be swung to cense a ritual space. These are often carried in processions.

Tree of Life A diagram consisting of 10 spheres connected by 22 paths showing the spiritual evolution of creation. It is central to the Qabalah, and is used by many western magicians as a kind of road map, showing where planetary or angelic powers may be located.

Warlock A term from the Anglo-Saxon "waerloga", a lie teller or deceiver, sometimes mistakenly used as a word for a male witch.

Wiccans Wiccans are initiated into the modern form of coven witchcraft, where they are led in their seasonal rituals by a High Priestess and High Priest. They are pagans in belief, but tend to use magic less than witches.

Widdershins Anticlockwise, from a Scottish dialect word. The Earth actually turns this way, making the Sun appear to move clockwise. Circles are walked widdershins to close down the power at the end of a ritual.

Witch A male or female person who uses the powers of Nature to work magic for healing or guidance. Witches may use ritual and celebrate the passing seasons but they are not necessarily pagans.

Yule This is the old Norse word, written "Jul", and meaning "wheel", for the time around the midwinter solstice. Celebrations include burning a Yule log to strengthen the power of the reborn sun.

Zener cards Special cards with clear shapes of a circle, square, cross, star as well as wavy lines, used to test extra sensory perception or psychic power.

Index